"Despite the central role of pornog
and psyches of millions of men, it
it thoughtfully and honestly: with each other, with women, and
perhaps most importantly, how rarely we examine its effects on us as
men. Robert Jensen's book does all of this. Agree or disagree with his
analyses or conclusions, this brave book challenges all of us to face
this crucial and sometimes painful subject with courage and hope."

—Jackson Katz, author of *The Macho Paradox*

"Thank you Robert Jensen! This is the message men need to hear. I
applaud Jensen for getting to the heart of the issue: men need to
stop using pornography and doing so would be a great benefit to
women, and to men as well. Jensen articulates the harmful effects
of pornography masterfully, and we believe this book and his work
is invaluable to the movement to end sexual violence against women
and children."

—Polly Poskin, Executive Director,
Illinois Coalition Against Sexual Assault

"Jensen's book is a shout to people who hate cruelty but think they can
choose their battles."

—Carol Bly, author of *Changing the Bully Who Rules the World*

PRAISE FOR **HEART OF WHITENESS**

"Very few white writers have been able to point out the pathological
nature of white privilege and supremacy with the eloquence of Robert
Jensen."

—Tim Wise, author of *White Like Me*

"Jensen's concise and thought-provoking book offers a variety of ways
for white Americans to abandon their unearned skin privilege and
rejoin the rest of humanity."

—Kel Munger, *Sacramento News and Review*

"With radical honesty, hard facts, and an abundance of insight and
compassion, Robert Jensen lays out strategies for recognizing and
dismantling white privilege—and helping others to do the same.
This text is more than just important; it's useful. Jensen demonstrates
again that he is a leading voice in the American quest for justice."

—Adam Mansbach, author of *Angry Black White Boy, or
The Miscegenation of Macon Detornay*

PRAISE FOR **CITIZENS OF THE EMPIRE**

"It is up to the citizens of the empire, Jensen says, to 'build movements that can transform people's opposition into political power.' That sounds like a tall order, but Jensen's use of personal anecdotes, analogies, and in-your-face common sense makes the reading easy and his request sound doable, even logical."

—Publishers Weekly

"Robert Jensen does more than challenge us to think and feel—he also encourages us to transform our lives."

—Norman Solomon, co-author of *Target Iraq*

"Robert Jensen supplies a much needed citizens' manual, that explains well the evasion of moral principles that underlie appeals to patriotism, and the differences between nominal and real free speech and a vibrant versus an empty and managed democracy."

—Edward S. Herman, co-author of *Manufacturing Consent*

getting off

[PORNOGRAPHY AND THE END OF MASCULINITY]

by Robert Jensen

South End Press
Cambridge, MA

Cover design: Design Action Collective.
Page design and production: South End Press Collective/Joey Fox.

Library of Congress Cataloging-in-Publication Data
Jensen, Robert, 1958-
  Getting off : pornography and the end of masculinity / by Robert Jensen.
     p. cm.
  Includes bibliographical references.
  ISBN 978-0-89608-776-7 (pbk. : alk. paper)
 1. Pornography--Moral and ethical aspects. 2. Pornography--Social
aspects. 3. Women--Crimes against. 4. Feminist theory. I. Title.

HQ471.J47 2007
306.77--dc22

                                   2007006615

Printed in Canada.
10 09 08 07   1 2 3 4 5 6 7 8 9

South End Press
7 Brookline Street, #1
Cambridge, MA 02139

http://www.southendpress.org
southend@southendpress.org

read. write. revolt.

This book is dedicated to the memories
of Andrea Dworkin and Sally Koplin.

Beatrice: What would happen if one woman told the truth about her life? The world would split open.

Houdini: It has. Now I'm going after it—all pieces.

—Muriel Rukeyser
Houdini: A Musical

table of contents

Our First Glance In The Mirror: The Rowdy Boys

I am at the Adult Entertainment Expo in Las Vegas in January 2005. At one of the 300 exhibitor booths on the floor of the Sands Expo Center is Tiffany Holiday, a woman who performs in pornographic movies. She is kissing and touching another female performer, and a crowd of men gathers around. There are rules for how much actual sexual activity can take place on the convention floor, and the two women are pushing the boundary. The crowd encourages them to go further.

The other woman leaves, and Tiffany begins to simulate masturbation, all the while talking dirty to the men gathered around her. The crowd swells to about 50 men. I'm stuck in the middle, holding a microphone for a documentary film crew. Emboldened by the size of the crowd, the men's chants for more-explicit sex grow louder and more boisterous. Holiday responds in kind, encouraging the men to tell her what they like. The exchange continues, intensifying to the point where the men are moving as a unit—like a mob.

Men's bodies are pressed against each other as each one vies for the best view of the woman's breasts, vagina, and anus. Many of the men are using cameras, camcorders, or cell phones to record the scene. It's difficult not to notice—not to feel—that the men pressed up against me have erections. It's difficult not to conclude that if there weren't security guards on the floor, these men would likely gang-rape Tiffany Holiday.

This is an expression of the dominant masculinity in the United States today. It is the masculinity of a mob, ready to rape.

introduction

masculinity

[ANDREA AND JIM]

B e a man.

It is a simple imperative, repeated over and over to men, starting when we are small boys. The phrase usually is connected to one man's demand that another man be "stronger," which is traditionally understood as the ability to suppress emotional reactions and channel that energy into controlling situations and establishing dominance.

Be a man, then, typically translates as: Surrender your humanity.

To be a man, then, is a bad trade. When we become men—when we accept the idea that there is something called masculinity to which we should conform—we exchange those aspects of ourselves that make life worth living for an endless struggle for power that, in the end, is illusory and destructive not only to others but to ourselves.

One response to this toxic masculinity has been to attempt to redefine what it means to be a man, to craft a kinder-and-gentler masculinity that might pose less of a threat to women and children and be more livable for men. But such a step is inadequate; our goal should not be to reshape masculinity but to eliminate it. The goal is liberation from the masculinity trap.

I spent my first 30 years trying to be a man, learning the rituals of masculinity. Like all men, I never completely mastered the game, but like most men I became proficient enough to get by. But like some men, somewhere in my gut I knew there was something wrong, not only with my ongoing failure to be "man enough" but with the whole concept of being a man. It didn't matter whether it was masculinity-as-domination or masculinity-as-sensitivity—it all felt inauthentic. In my gut, it felt wrong. I spent 30 years repressing that gut feeling, to the detriment of myself and those around me.

I've spent the past 20 years trying to change, to chart some course toward being not a man but a human being. This book is about that process, told in three different voices. Part of what I have learned comes from my work as a researcher and professor in the university; I will draw on data and theory (which need not be boring or irrelevant, though they often are). Part of my knowledge is based in political activism within a feminist movement, particularly the feminist anti-pornography movement; I cannot imagine making sense of this subject without feminism (which is a gift to men, not a threat). And, finally, part of this is simply my story, as a relatively ordinary man living in an ordinary world; I try to look at my own life as honestly as possible (which may sound scary, because it is).[1] Because this book moves between research, politics, and the personal, I want to start at the moment when those three came together for me.

In 1988 I left my career as a newspaper reporter and editor to begin a doctoral program in media ethics and law at the University of Minnesota. My interest in the law and philosophy concerning freedom of expression led me to the feminist critique of men's violence and the sexual-exploitation industries, including pornography, which at that moment was one of the most controversial issues in First Amendment juris- prudence. I came to that study as a fairly normal guy with typi- cal experiences as a pornography user through childhood and early adulthood, and I had fairly typical liberal/libertarian ideas about pornography—to each his own/so long as it's between consenting adults/one man's art is another's pornography, and so on. But I also had a nagging feeling that there were questions I should ask myself, personal spaces I should push into, ideas I should explore.

ANDREA DWORKIN

When I started graduate school, I had a vague recollection of who Andrea Dworkin was from the political struggle over a feminist anti-pornography civil rights ordinance in Minneapolis five years earlier. During that struggle, she was routinely re- ferred to by opponents as a man-hating feminist dyke, which was the image I carried with me as I started to read her work. One of the first things I read was a speech she gave to a men's group in 1983, "I Want a Twenty-Four-Hour Truce During Which There Is No Rape." The title was her response to the question, "Well, just what do women want from men?" Just give us women one day of rest, she said, "one day in which no new bodies are piled up, one day in which no new agony is added to the old."[2] Her request was powerful because of its grim simplicity; it forced us to recognize that we are light-years away from being able to imagine a day without rape.

Her critique of men's violence was blunt, honest, and impossible to ignore. But more important to me as I read was not the way in which she critiqued men and held us accountable, but that her love for men was so evident. This was a woman I had been told hated men, and yet running through her talk was a profound compassion for men, and by extension, for me. Here's what she told those men in 1983:

> I don't believe rape is inevitable or natural. If I did, I would have no reason to be here. If I did, my political practice would be different than it is. Have you ever wondered why we [women] are not just in armed combat against you? It's not because there's a shortage of kitchen knives in this country. It is because we believe in your humanity, against all the evidence.[3]

It started to become clear: Dworkin wanted to help men transcend masculinity, in part because she believed in people—men and women—and was fueled by a love and compassion that went deeper than I had ever seen in a public political person. She wanted to help us, though, not just for our sake but to stop men's violence against women. She wanted an end to the harassment, rape, battery, child sexual assault. And she knew that required men to change, to save ourselves. In that same speech, she challenged men to take that responsibility:

> We do not want to do the work of helping you to believe in your humanity. We cannot do it anymore. We have always tried. We have been repaid with systematic exploitation and systematic abuse. You are going to have to do this yourselves from now on and you know it.[4]

That was the first time Andrea Dworkin's writing brought me to tears. That was the beginning of recognizing that the path to resolving my long-standing uneasiness about masculinity had already been charted by radical feminists. But that recognition had yet to take form. I had no idea how to move forward, and I had no models for what it meant to be a man working in a feminist context. Then I got lucky.

JIM KOPLIN

As I started to work on academic projects on pornography and feminism, I learned there was a group in Minneapolis, Organizing Against Pornography (OAP), that presented public programs on the subject. When I called, the group's volunteer office manager, Jim Koplin, answered the phone. I explained that I wanted to know more about the group as part of my research, and Jim at first was somewhat reserved in response (later he explained that some of the calls they got requesting information were from political opponents trying to undermine OAP's work, hence his hesitation). Once he decided my interest was honest, he was willing to tell me more about the group and his role in it, and we agreed on an early-morning breakfast meeting.

Jim, a psychology professor who had returned to his native Minnesota after early retirement from academic life, was at that point the only man regularly working with OAP, a women-run radical feminist organization. He explained that he saw his role as offering skills that the group needed, under the direction of women. Men who wanted to do such work need not be passive wallflowers afraid to ever speak or assert themselves, he said, but we should realize that feminist insights are grounded in the experience and knowledge of women. The role of men was to avoid the temptation to want to assume leadership and instead listen, learn, and find appropriate ways to contribute to the collective effort.

As with reading Andrea Dworkin, that first experience with Jim was a bit unsettling to my stereotypes. Here was someone trained as an academic who didn't seem to spend all his time proving how smart he was, and a man who apparently felt no need to fight to be in charge. He had dedicated his life to learning and to transforming that knowledge into action, in an ethical and political framework that made intuitive sense to me, though it was unfamiliar at that moment. I had a sense my world was changing—for the better—but I didn't understand much of it.

My conversations with Jim continued, morphing into a regular weekly coffee meeting during which we talked about intellectual, political, and personal issues. At some point in that process, it became clear that I wanted to not only study the issue of pornography but also participate politically in the feminist movement against that form of the sexual exploitation of women. I had met the women at OAP and saw a place for myself in its activism. That's when Jim sat me down for "the talk." He told me I was welcome to be part of OAP, but I had to be clear about my motivations.

"If you want to be part of this because you want to save women, we don't want you," he said. At first I was confused—wasn't the point of critiquing the sexual exploitation of women in pornography to help women? Yes, Jim explained, but too many men who get involved in such work see themselves as knights in shining armor, riding in like the hero to save women, and they usually turn out not to be trustworthy allies. They are in it for themselves, not to challenge masculinity but to play out the role of heroic man in a new, pseudo-feminist context. You have to be in it for yourself, but in a different way, he said.

"You have to be here to save your own life," Jim told me.

I didn't understand exactly what he meant at that moment, but something about those words resonated in my gut. This is what feminism offered men—not just a way to help those being hurt, but a way to understand that the same system of male dominance that hurt so many women also made it impossible for men to be fully human.

THE STRUGGLE

Andrea and Jim made it clear to me: I could settle for being a man, or I could struggle to become a human being.

If I settled, the rewards would be obvious but the unseen costs were huge. I could take my place in the hierarchy with reasonable expectations of a materially comfortable life and status in the world, but I would continue to be nagged by the feeling that I was not man enough. I would constantly be fitting myself into someone else's notion of what it meant to be a man, and since I had never found a definition of masculinity that made sense to me, whatever masculinity I donned would always be ill-fitting.

If I struggled, I couldn't predict how difficult and painful the road would be, but I would be taking steps toward liberation. I would be giving up concrete rewards in favor of long-term benefits that were difficult to describe.

Andrea and Jim made it clear to me: It was worth it to struggle, not because it was easy but because it was the only way to save myself. Once I was aware of the choice, there really was no choice. Living cluelessly—unaware that there is an alternative to the conventional life handed to us—takes its toll. If we see the alternatives and realize we have a choice, but then turn our backs on it, we have condemned ourselves to a life of endless regret.

Still, nearly 20 years later, I cannot be glib about that choice. Not only is the struggle more painful than I ever imagined, but my failures along the way became even more difficult to confront. As I write this, that pain is not fully resolved and my failures are still far too frequent and wrenching. There are times I wish I didn't know what I know, days I feel as if I am drowning. But there has never been a moment in which I wish I had chosen otherwise. Jim's consistency and Andrea's memory make it easy to continue the work, even when I feel broken by it.

Jim remains a friend and ally 20 years later. As I moved into a more public role as a writer and speaker about pornography and other progressive political issues, I have relied on his knowledge, judgment, and support. I have met other men in feminist work, many who proved to be untrustworthy but also many whose commitment and courage renew my sense of hope. Among them, Jim remains my model of how people in positions of privilege can work with integrity to undermine those systems of power and privilege.

Andrea died on April 9, 2005, after struggling for several years with a variety of health problems that I assume were in some way related to her political work. Andrea had put her heart and soul and body on the line for a simple principle: Women matter as much as men, and men have it in them to recognize that and change. She remained open to the pain of both women and men in order to understand the complex way in which patriarchy can destroy women and constrain men. Whatever one thinks of her politics, it's impossible not to respect the courage with which she faced that pain. And it's hard not to recognize that it was that pain which, in part, killed her.

I first heard of Andrea's death over the phone from my friend and co-author Gail Dines. I recall the sinking feeling in my stomach when she told me. My first words in response were, "Oh Gail, what are we going to do now?"

REFUSING TO LOOK AWAY

What we did, of course, was to keep on. Gail and I—along with others who are committed to a feminist critique of the pornographic world—have continued to work on research, writing, and organizing. It sounds clichéd, but it's what Andrea would have expected of us.

I believe Andrea was the first person to understand that the contemporary pornography industry and the images it produces are a place to look squarely into the consequences of patriarchy and masculinity. To look honestly, I believe, is to open oneself up to the pain that Andrea articulated. That is not an easy task. It's tempting to want to look away or look only at the surface, and most people do. But to do that is to abandon our obligation to others and a duty to ourselves.

This book is the product of nearly 20 years of work, activism, and struggle—intellectual, political, and personal. I don't hold out my experience as completely typical, my path as a model, or my answers as universally applicable. But I'm pretty sure that the questions I have are important. I am sure that no matter how difficult it is to look at what pornography tells us about ourselves, we have to look.

Can we bear to look? Can we afford not to?

pornography
[THE PARADOX IN THE MIRROR]

After an intense three hours, the workshop on pornography I have been leading is winding down. The 40 women all work at a center that serves battered women and rape survivors. These are the women on the front lines, the ones who answer the 24-hour hotline and work one-on-one with victims. They counsel women who have just been raped, help women who have been beaten, and nurture children who have been abused. These women have heard and seen it all. No matter how brutal a story might be, they have experienced or heard one even more brutal; there is no way to one-up them on stories of men's violence. But after three hours of information, analysis, and discussion of the commercial heterosexual pornography industry, many of these women are drained. Sadness hangs over the room.

Near the end of the session, one woman who had been quiet starts to speak. Throughout the workshop she had held herself in tightly, her arms wrapped around herself. She talks for some time, and then apologizes for rambling. There is no need to apologize; she is articulating what many feel. She talks about her own life, about what she has learned in the session and how it has made her feel, about her anger and sadness.

Finally, she says: "This hurts. It just hurts so much."

Everyone is quiet as the words sink in. Slowly the conversation restarts, and the women talk more about how they feel, how they will use the information, what it will mean to their work and in their lives. The session ends, but her words hang in the air.

It hurts.

It hurts to know that no matter who you are as a woman, you can be reduced to a thing to be penetrated, and that men will buy movies about that, and that in many of those movies your humiliation will be the central theme. It hurts to know that so much of the pornography that men are buying fuses sexual desire with cruelty.

It hurts women, and men like it, and it hurts just to know that.

Even these women, who have found ways to cope with the injuries from male violence in other places, struggle with that pornographic reality. It is one thing to deal with acts, even extremely violent acts. It is another to know the thoughts, ideas, and fantasies that lie behind those acts.

People routinely assume that pornography is such a difficult and divisive issue because it's about sex. In fact, this culture struggles unsuccessfully with pornography because it is about men's cruelty to women, and the pleasure men sometimes take in that cruelty. And that is much more difficult for people—men and women—to face.

WHY IT HURTS

This doesn't mean that all men take sexual pleasure in cruelty. It doesn't mean that all women reject pornography. There is great individual variation in the human species, but there also are patterns in any society. And when those patterns tell us things about ourselves and the world in which we live that are difficult, we often want to look away.

Mirrors can be dangerous, and pornography is a mirror.

Pornography as a mirror shows us how men see women. Not all men, of course—but the ways in which many men who accept the conventional conception of masculinity see women. It is unsettling to look into that mirror.

A story about that: I am out with two heterosexual women friends. Both are feminists in their 30s, and both are successful in their careers. Both are smart and strong, and both have had trouble finding male partners who aren't scared by their intelligence and strength. We are talking about men and women, about relationships. As is often the case, I am told that I am too hard on men. The implication is that after so many years of working in the radical feminist critique of the sex industry and sexual violence, I have become jaded, too mired in the dark side of male sexuality. I contend that I am simply trying to be honest. We go back and forth, in a friendly discussion.

Finally, I tell my friends that I can settle this with a description of one website. I say to them: "If you want me to, I will tell you about this site. I won't tell you if you don't want to hear this. But if you want me to continue, don't blame me." They look at each other; they hesitate. They ask me to explain.

Some months before that someone had forwarded to me an e-mail about a pornography site that the person thought I should take a look at—slutbus.com. It's a website to sell videos of the Slut Bus. Here's the Slut Bus concept:

A few men who appear to be in their 20s drive around in a minivan with a video camera. They ask women if they want a ride. Once in the van, the women are asked if they would be willing to have sex on camera for money. The women do. When the sex is over, the women get out of the van and one of the men hands the women a wad of bills as payment. Just as she reaches for the money, the van drives off, leaving her on the side of the road looking foolish. There are trailers for ten videos on the website. All appear to use the same "plot" structure.

There are men who buy videos with that simple message: Women are for sex. Women can be bought for sex. But in the end, women are not even worth paying for sex. They don't even deserve to be bought. They just deserve to be fucked, and left on the side of the road, with postadolescent boys laughing as they drive away—while men at home watch, become erect, masturbate, obtain sexual pleasure, and ejaculate, and then turn off the DVD player and go about their lives. There are other companies that produce similar videos. There's bangbus.com, which leaves women by the side of the road after sex in the Bang Bus. And bangboat.com. And on it goes.

I look at my friends and tell them: "You realize what I just described is relatively tame. There are things far more brutal and humiliating than that, you know."

We sit quietly, until one of them says, "That wasn't fair."

I know that it wasn't fair. What I had told them was true, and they had asked me to tell them. But it wasn't fair to push it. If I were them, if I were a woman, I wouldn't want to know that. Life is difficult enough without knowing things like that, without having to face that one lives in a society in which no matter who you are—as an individual, as a person with hopes and dreams, with strengths and weaknesses—you are something to be fucked and laughed at and left on the side of the road by men. Because you are a woman.

"I'm sorry," I said. "But you asked."

In a society in which so many men are watching so much pornography, this is why we can't bear to see it for what it is: Pornography forces women to face up to how men see them. And pornography forces men to face up to what we have become. The result is that no one wants to talk about what is in the mirror. Although few admit it, lots of people are afraid of pornography. The liberal/libertarian supporters who celebrate pornography are afraid to look honestly at what it says about our culture. The conservative opponents are afraid that pornography undermines their attempts to keep sex boxed into narrow categories.

Feminist critics are afraid, too—but for different reasons. Feminists are afraid because of what they see in the mirror, because of what pornography tells us about the world in which we live. That fear is justified. It's a sensible fear that leads many to want to change the culture.

Pornography has become normalized, mainstreamed. The values that drive the Slut Bus also drive the larger culture. As a *New York Times* story put it, "Pornography isn't just for dirty old men anymore." Well, it never really was just for dirty men, or old men, or dirty old men. But now that fact is out in the open. That same story quotes a magazine writer who also has written a pornography script: "People just take porn in stride these days. There's nothing dangerous about sex anymore."[1] The editorial director of *Playboy*, who says that his company has "an emphasis on party," tells potential advertisers: "We're in the mainstream."[2]

There never was anything dangerous about sex, of course. The danger isn't in sex, but in a particular conception of sex in patriarchy. And the way sex is done in pornography is becoming more and more cruel and degrading at the same time that pornography is becoming more normalized than ever. That's the paradox.

THE PARADOX OF PORNOGRAPHY

First, imagine what we could call the cruelty line—the measure of the level of overt cruelty toward, and degradation of, women in contemporary mass-marketed pornography. That line is heading up, sharply.

Second, imagine the normalization line—the measure of the acceptance of pornography in the mainstream of contemporary culture. That line also is on the way up, equally sharply.

If pornography is increasingly cruel and degrading, why is it increasingly commonplace instead of more marginalized? In a society that purports to be civilized, wouldn't we expect most people to reject sexual material that becomes ever more dismissive of the humanity of women? How do we explain the simultaneous appearance of more, and increasingly more intense, ways to humiliate women sexually and the rising popularity of the films that present those activities?

As is often the case, this paradox can be resolved by recognizing that one of the assumptions is wrong. Here, it's the assumption that US society routinely rejects cruelty and degradation. In fact, the United States is a nation that has no serious objection to cruelty and degradation. Think of the way we accept the use of brutal weapons in war that kill civilians, or the way we accept the death penalty, or the way we accept crushing economic inequality. There is no paradox in the steady mainstreaming of an intensely cruel pornography. This is a culture with a well-developed legal regime that generally protects individuals' rights and freedoms, and yet it also is a strikingly cruel culture in the way it accepts brutality and inequality. The pornographers are not a deviation from the norm. Their presence in the mainstream shouldn't be surprising, because they represent mainstream values: the logic of domination and subordination that is central to patriarchy, hyper-patriotic nationalism, white supremacy, and a predatory corporate capitalism.

Pornography-as-a-mirror can take us beyond sex into even more disturbing territory, which leads back to masculinity.

masculinity

where we are stuck

[PLAYING KING OF THE HILL]

ACT I

I am having dinner on a Thursday night in a restaurant in New York's Greenwich Village with Robert Wosnitzer and Miguel Picker, two friends I'm working with on a documentary on pornography. We've had a long day and are happy to unwind. Near the end of our meal, I'm increasingly aware of the rising volume from a nearby table, where three college-age men and a woman are talking and laughing just a bit too loudly. As it becomes harder to shut out their conversation, it becomes clear that much of the talk is about sex. The alpha male of the group (who is the boyfriend of the woman) is holding forth to the other two men about how to maneuver women into bed, including tips on the use of alcohol and a little bit of force when necessary.

As my friends and I get up to leave, I catch the eye of the woman, inquiring silently whether her situation would be improved if we stopped by the table and said something to the men. I read, or more likely misread, her expression as an invitation to do so. I trail behind my friends and stop at the table, trying to suggest—in lighthearted fashion that isn't too confrontational—that their conversation was not only inappropriate in a public place but unacceptable anywhere. The men don't take the critique well, and the discussion heats up a bit.

Finally, the alpha male makes a move to settle things by going for what he presumes to be the ultimate insult: "All I know," he says, smirking, "is that I'm going home with her (pointing to his girlfriend) and you're leaving with two guys."

Check.

I respond: "Please don't take this personally, but I just don't find you sexually attractive. I'm sure there will be a man who someday will, but it's just not happening for me."

Checkmate.

He accuses me of being gay. I accept the label and respond by telling him that, as a gay man, I can see into him and recognize him as gay as well. Not a smart move on my part, it turns out.

I quickly realize that things aren't likely to end happily, and I make my way to the door. One of his buddies follows me and, just as I'm leaving, says, "It's time for you to get the hell out of here." My hand is on the first of two exit doors, pushing it open. I say to him, "Where does it look like I'm going?" He grabs me and reiterates the command to leave. I reflexively push back. "Listen, son," I start to say, reacting like an old guy to the 25 years between us. He's bigger than me but drunk. As I push back, he starts to fall. I head for the second door just about the time my friends have come back to pull me out if necessary. As I'm walking on the sidewalk outside, the other two young men have joined their friend in the doorway, cursing me with instructions not to come back, advice I fully intend to take. My friends hustle me away, walking quickly to get clear of the place just in case the men decide to follow. Robert explains that he grew up around guys like that. "Those are the kind of guys who carry baseball bats in the trunks of their cars," he says. "You have to be careful. They like this. They like to fight."

Once we're out of range, Robert and Miguel turn to me and, appropriately, explain why I had better not pull such a stunt again. They count the four stupid men in that encounter: The alpha male, his two buddies, and me. They are right, of course. The fact that I wasn't as crude and violent as the other three hardly absolves me. I had taken an unnecessary risk, putting others in a situation where they may have had to fight or be hurt, and I had done it out of the same macho posturing. Once engaged, I refused to back down, even though there was nothing positive that could come of the encounter and a real risk.

ACT II

The next day, I fly to an academic conference. I am still somewhat shaken by the previous night, not so much by the potential for violence (though I'm not a particularly physically courageous person) but by my own misjudgment and the lessons in that for me. It's not what I learned about the world the previous night that upset me, but what I learned about myself.

So, I'm looking forward to a low-key interaction with other academics, who are usually pretty harmless. At the end of that evening I'm in the hotel bar with one female and two male professors. We all seem to be of similar intellectual and political leanings, and the conversation finds its way to contemporary progressive political movements, especially the antiwar movement. I offer an analysis of the state of organizing in the United States, which one of the men takes issue with. I respond to his critique, and all of a sudden the conversation kicks into overdrive. He comes back to my points even harder, getting visibly upset. He turns the discussion from an argument about issues to an attack on me, suggesting that I lack his experience and knowledge (he's about a decade older).

With the previous night's conflict on my mind, I back off a bit, responding to his arguments but trying to lower the intensity; I am not in the mood for a fight, even verbally. He presses forward even more forcefully. At this point, the other two people at the table are visibly uncomfortable. I move to end the conversation, suggesting that some of our disagreements can't be resolved, that we are both arguing based on our hunches about complex processes, and that perhaps there is no point in pushing it. At this point, I don't care about winning the argument and want to end an exchange that is uncomfortable to the others for no good reason—no baseball bats are going to come out in this encounter, but no one is learning anything from this. He pushes one more time, implicitly demanding that I surrender to his greater knowledge and insight. One of the others finds it intolerable and leaves, and the tension finally dissipates. The conversation returns to a lower level, but it's impossible to go back, and we quickly go our separate ways.

ACT III

Sunday morning I'm on a plane heading home. Across the aisle from me is a man most easily described as a stereotypical computer nerd, in appearance and activity. He opens his laptop once we hit our cruising altitude and is buried in it the rest of the flight until the female flight attendant comes by during our descent to remind him to turn off his electronic device, which might interfere with the plane's navigational equipment. He ignores the first warning. She comes by again with a polite second warning, which he also ignores. Finally, it's three strikes and he's out. She stands over him and explains—politely, but with an edge in her voice that says, "enough screwing around, buddy"—that he must shut off the computer. I'm chuckling at the scene, until I see that he's angry. After the experience of the past couple of days, I'm not eager to be in the middle of another public expression of male dominance.

He looks up at her, his facial muscles tightening, appearing ready to tell her off, but he wisely holds his tongue. She holds her ground, and he finally backs off and powers down the laptop. Once she's convinced he's turned it off, she moves on. He sits, quiet but clearly struggling to control his rage. When she is out of hearing range, he looks over at me and, just loud enough for me but no one else to hear, mutters, "Bitch." A trace of a smile comes to his lips, and he turns away from me before I can respond. In his mind, he has won. A woman had been in a position of some small authority over him and had forced him to obey her command. But in the end, she's just a bitch, and he's still a man.

Masculinity in three acts: Attempts at dominance through (1) force and humiliation, (2) words and argument, and (3) raw insults. Three episodes about the ways masculinity does men in, neatly played out during one long weekend. By the time I get home, I am tired. I am sad. It feels like there are few ways out.

DEFINITIONS: SEX AND GENDER

To talk about masculinity, it's necessary to be precise about how we name and understand categories around sex and gender. That means being clear about some very simple things.

There are three categories of biological human sex identity: male, female, and intersexed.[1] The vast majority of humans are born with distinctly male or female reproductive systems, sexual characteristics, and/or chromosomal structure, and there is some segment (the percentage in this category would depend on what degree of ambiguity marks the category) born with reproductive or sexual anatomy that doesn't fit the definitions of female or male.[2] These categories are biological—based on the material reality of who can potentially reproduce with whom—

and exist independent of any particular cultural understanding of them. That is what typically is called "sex."

Beyond the category of "sex" (the biological differences between males and females) is "gender" (the non-biological meaning societies create out of sex differences). Gender plays out in a variety of ways, including gender roles (assigning males and females to different social, political, or economic roles); gender norms (expecting males and females to comply with different norms of behavior and appearance); gendered traits and virtues (assuming that males and females will be psychologically or morally different from each other); gender identity (a person's internal sense of gender—of masculinity, femininity, or something in between—which may not be how others perceive the person); and gender symbolism (using gender in the description of animals, inanimate objects, or ideas).[3]

About those in the sex category male, we commonly speak of a man who is masculine and has (or should have) the qualities of masculinity. About those in the sex category female, we speak of a woman who is feminine and has (or should have) the qualities of femininity. For someone in the sex category intersexed, we have no terminology, and traditionally this culture has attempted to force such people into either the male or female categories, typically with negative consequences.[4]

There's one gendered term associated with males that's far more prevalent than the corresponding term for females: "manhood." In this culture, we talk in everyday conversation about manhood and what it means. We talk of womanhood far less frequently; both words are in the dictionary, but only one is part of routine vocabularies. We rarely hear someone challenge the womanhood of a female. We routinely hear males challenging each other's manhood. Why is that?

THE DOMINANT CONCEPTION OF MASCULINITY

I'm fond of many human persons who are male, but I don't much care for men, manhood, and masculinity. Later I will explain in more detail why we have to leave those terms behind, but for now I want to examine the meaning of "man," "manhood," and "masculinity" in the world in which I was born, raised, and still live. In other words, what do those terms mean in our lived experience?

The dominant conception of masculinity in US culture is easily summarized: Men are assumed to be naturally competitive and aggressive, and being a "real man" is therefore marked by the struggle for control, conquest, and domination. A man looks at the world, sees what he wants, and takes it.

Those men who don't measure up are suspect—they are wimps, sissies, fags, girls. The worst insult one man can hurl at another—whether among boys on the playground or corporate executives in the boardroom—is the accusation that a man is like a woman (or is gay, which is assumed to be too much like a woman). Although the culture acknowledges that men can in some situations have gendered traits traditionally associated with women (such as caring, compassion, tenderness), in the end it is men's strength-expressed-as-toughness that defines us and must trump any woman-like softness. Those aspects of masculinity must prevail for a man to be a real man.

To identify this dominant definition of what it means to be a man is not to suggest that every male adopts it. Scholars and activists often talk of "masculinities," plural—the idea that different men may fashion different conceptions of what it means to be a man, with varying degrees of success. That's certainly true, but it doesn't change the fact that there is a dominant conception of masculinity, to which virtually all males are exposed and with which a significant percentage (likely a substantial majority) identify in some fashion—including me. Nor does it change the fact that many men who claim to be challenging the dominant conception of masculinity are simply putting a new face on the same system, the key components of which are

» the avoidance of things too closely connected to women/femininity;

» the struggle for supremacy in interpersonal relationships and social situations; and

» the repression of emotions connected to women/femininity (The phrasing of this is crucial, for men do not repress all emotion; in certain situations, men freely express anger, for example.)

KING OF THE HILL

The object of the children's game King of the Hill is to be the one who remains on top of the hill (or, if not an actual hill, a large pile of anything or the center of any designated area). To do that, one has to repel those who challenge the king's supremacy. The king has to push away all the other kids who charge the hill. That can be done in a friendly spirit with an understanding that a minimal amount of force will be used by all, or it can be violent and vicious, with both the king and the challengers allowed to use any means necessary. Games that start with such a friendly understanding can often turn violent and vicious. This scenario is also used in some video games, in which a player tries to control a specific area for a predetermined amount of time.

In my experience, both male and female children can, and did, play King of the Hill, but it was overwhelmingly a game of male children. It's one of the games that train male children to be men. No matter who is playing, it is a game of masculinity. King of the Hill reveals one essential characteristic of the dominant conception of masculinity: No one is ever safe, and everyone loses something.

Most obviously, this King of the Hill masculinity is dangerous for women. It leads men to seek to control "their" women and define their own pleasure in that control, which leads to epidemic levels of rape and battery. But this view of masculinity is toxic for men as well.

One thing is immediately obvious about King of the Hill masculinity: Not everyone can win. In fact, by its very definition, there's only one real man at any given moment. In a system based on hierarchy, there can be only one person at the top. There's only one King of the Hill.

In this conception of masculinity, men are in constant struggle with each other for dominance. Every other man must in some way be subordinated to the king, but even the king can't feel too comfortable—he has to be nervous about who is coming up that hill to get him. This isn't just a game, of course. A friend who once worked on Wall Street, one of the preeminent sites of masculine competition in the business world, described coming to work as like "walking into a knife fight when all the good spots along the wall were taken." Every day you faced the possibility of getting killed—figuratively, in business terms—and there was no spot you could stand where your back was covered. This is masculinity lived as endless competition and threat.

Whatever the benefits of it, whatever power it gives one over others, it's also exhausting and, in the end, unfulfilling.

No one man created this system. Perhaps no man, if given a real choice, would choose it. But we live our lives in this system, and it deforms men, narrowing our emotional range and depth and limiting our capacity to experience rich connections with others—not just with women and children, but with other men. Such connections require vulnerability but make life meaningful. The Man Who Would Be King is the Man Who Is Broken and Alone.

That toxic masculinity hurts men doesn't mean it's equally harmful for men and women. As feminists have long pointed out, there's a big difference between women dealing with the constant threat of being raped, beaten, and killed by the men in their lives, and men not being able to cry. But we can see that the short-term material gains that men derive from patriarchy—the name for this system of male dominance—are not adequate compensation for what we men give up in the long haul, which is to surrender part of our humanity to the project of dominance.

This doesn't mean, of course, that in this world all men have it easy. As a result of other systems of dominance and oppression—white supremacy, heterosexism, predatory corporate capitalism—men of color, gay men, poor and working-class men suffer in various ways. A feminist analysis doesn't preclude us from understanding those problems but in fact helps us see them more clearly.

WHAT FEMINISM IS AND ISN'T TO ME

Each fall in my seminar class for first-year students at the University of Texas, I lead a discussion about gender politics that will sound familiar to many teachers. I ask the students about their opinions about various gender issues, such as equal pay, sexual harassment, men's violence, and gender roles. Most of the women and some of the men express views that would be called feminist. But when I ask how many identify as feminists, out of the 15 students in any semester, no more than 3 (always women) have ever claimed the label. When I ask why, the typical answers are not about the political positions of feminism but the perception that feminism is weird and that weird people are feminists.

This pattern is no doubt connected to the assault on feminism in the mainstream culture, captured most succinctly in the term "femi-nazi" made popular by right-wing radio host Rush Limbaugh. One response to this assault by some feminists has been to find a least-common-denominator definition of the term, to reassure both men and women that feminism doesn't really aim to undermine established gender norms and isn't threatening to men. I believe that to be the wrong strategy. If feminism is to make a meaningful difference in the sex/gender crisis we face and contribute to a broader social change so desperately needed, I believe it must be clear in its challenge to the existing order—and that inevitably will be threatening to many men, at least at first. Feminism, then, should get more radical than ever.

In general, the term "radical" conjures up images of extremes, of danger, of people eager to tear things down. But "radical" has another meaning—from the Latin, for "root." Radical solutions are the ones that get to the root of the problem. When the systems in which we live are in crisis, the most honest confrontations with those systems have to be radical. At first glance, that honesty will seem frightening. Looking deeper, one can see that it is the radical ideas that offer hope, a way out of the crisis.

Because these ideas are denigrated in the dominant culture, it's important to define them. By "feminist," I mean an analysis of the ways in which women are oppressed as a class in this society—the ways in which men as a class hold more power, and how those differences in power systematically disadvantage women in the public and private spheres. Gender oppression plays out in different ways depending on social location, which makes it crucial to understand men's oppression of women in connection with other systems of oppression—heterosexism, racism, class privilege, and histories of colonial and postcolonial domination.

By "radical feminist," I mean the analysis of the ways that in this patriarchal system in which we live, one of the key sites of this oppression—one key method of domination—is sexuality. Two of the most well-known women who articulated a radical feminist view have been central to the feminist critique of pornography—the writer Andrea Dworkin[5] and Catharine MacKinnon,[6] a lawyer and law professor. The feminist philosophy and politics that have shaped my thinking are most clearly articulated by those two and others with similar views.[7]

What I learned from this radical feminism is not just a way of critiquing men's domination of women but also a broader approach to understanding systems of power and oppression. Feminism is not the only way into a broader critique of the many types of oppression, of course, but it is one important way, and for me it was the first route into such a framework. My real political education started on the issue of gender and from there moved to issues of racial and economic injustice, the imperialist wars that flow out of that injustice, and the ecological crisis. Each system of power and oppression is unique in its own way, but there are certain features they have in common. Here's my summary:

How do we explain the fact that most people's stated philosophical and theological systems are rooted in concepts of justice, equality, and the inherent dignity of all people, yet we allow violence, exploitation, and oppression to flourish? Only a small percentage of people in any given society are truly sociopaths, engaging in cruel and oppressive behavior openly and with relish. Feminism helped me understand the complex process, which tends to work like this:

» The systems and structures in which we live are hierarchical.

» Hierarchical systems and structures deliver to those in the dominant class certain privileges, pleasures, and material benefits.

» People are typically hesitant to give up such privileges, pleasures, and benefits.

» But those benefits clearly come at the expense of those in the subordinated classes.

» Given the widespread acceptance of basic notions of equality and human rights, the existence of hierarchy has to be justified in some way other than crass self-interest.

» One of the most persuasive arguments for systems of domination and subordination is that they are "natural."

So, oppressive systems work hard to make it appear that the hierarchy—and the disparity in power and resources that flow from hierarchy—is natural and, therefore, beyond modification. If men are naturally smarter and stronger than women, then patriarchy is inevitable and justifiable. If white people are naturally smarter and more virtuous than people of color, then white supremacy is inevitable and justifiable. If rich people are naturally smarter and harder working than poor people, then economic injustice is inevitable and justifiable. And if human beings have special status in the universe, justified either on theological or biological grounds, then humans' right to extract from the rest of Creation whatever they like is inevitable and justifiable.

For unjust hierarchies, and the illegitimate authority that is exercised in them, maintaining their own naturalness is essential. Not surprisingly, people in the dominant class exercising the power gravitate easily to such a view. And because of their power to control key storytelling institutions (especially education and mass communication), they can fashion a story about the world that leads some portion of the people in the subordinate classes to internalize the ideology.

For me, feminism gave me a way to see through not only male dominance, but all the systems of illegitimate authority. I saw the fundamental strategy they held in common, and saw that if we could move into a space in which we were true to our stated ideals, we would reject those systems as anti-human. All these systems cause suffering beyond the telling. All of them must be resisted. The connections between them must be understood.

ENFORCING MASCULINITY

Systems of oppression are interlocked and enmeshed; perhaps the classic example is the way in which white men identify black men as a threat to the sexual purity of white women, requiring white men to maintain control over both black people and white women. While keeping those connections in mind, we can train our attention on how each individual power system operates. This book attempts such a focus on masculinity. The King of the Hill masculinity I have described is articulated and enforced in a variety of places in contemporary culture, most notably athletics, the military, and business, with underpinnings in the dominant monotheistic religions. We can look at all those arenas and see how masculinity-as-dominance plays out. In all those endeavors, the quality of relationships and human values become secondary to control that leads to victory, conquest, and closing the deal.

We teach our boys that to be a man is to be tough, to be acquisitive, to be competitive, to be aggressive. We congratulate them when they make a tough hit on the football field that takes out an opponent. We honor them in parades when they return from slaughtering the enemy abroad. We put them on magazine covers when they destroy business competitors and make millions by putting people out of work. In short, we train boys to be cruel, to ignore the feelings of others, to be violent.

US culture's most admired male heroes reflect those characteristics: They most often are men who take charge rather than seek consensus, seize power rather than look for ways to share it, and are willing to be violent to achieve their goals. Victory is sweet. Conquest gives a sense of power. And after closing the deal, the sweet sense of power lingers.

Look around in the contemporary United States, and masculinity is paraded in front of us, sometimes in displays that border on self-parody:

» George W. Bush dons a flight suit and lands on an aircraft carrier; the self-proclaimed "war president" announces victory (albeit somewhat prematurely). John Kerry, fearing a masculinity gap, serves up a hunting photo op in the 2004 campaign to show that not only does he have combat experience that Bush lacks but still likes to fire a weapon.

» Arnold Schwarzenegger moves from action-movie hero to governor of California, denigrating opponents he deems insufficiently tough as "girly men."

» Donald Trump, a businessman famous mostly for being famous and attracting conventionally attractive female partners, boosts a sagging public image with *The Apprentice*, a television show that pits young wannabe executives against each other in cutthroat competition.

And then there is sex, where victory, conquest, and dealing come together, typically out of public view. Masculinity played out in sexual relationships, straight or gay, brings King of the Hill into our most intimate spaces. Again, not every man in every sexual situation plays out this dominance, but the pattern exists. When I speak to mixed groups about these subjects, I often describe the sex-as-dominance paradigm, and then I ask the women in the room if they have any experience with men behaving in such fashion. There is considerable rolling of the eyes and many exasperated sighs at that point. I present it in a lighthearted fashion because to do otherwise makes most mixed audiences very nervous.

And then there is pornography, which brings the private imposition of masculinity into public, putting King of the Hill sex onto the screen.

PORNOGRAPHY'S WHISPER TO MEN

We think of the call of pornography as crass, like that of a carnival barker. Like the neon lights of Times Square in its pornographic heyday. Men go to buy pornography in the "red light district," the "combat zone." Pornography seems to shout out at us, crudely.

But in reality, pornography speaks to men in a whisper. We pretend to listen to the barker shouting about women, but that is not the draw. What brings us back, over and over, is the voice in our ears, the soft voice that says, "It's okay, you really are a man, you really can be a man, and if you come into my world, it will all be there, and it will all be easy."

Pornography knows men's weakness. It speaks to that weakness, softly. Pornography ends up being about men's domination of women and about the ugly ways that men will take pleasure. But for most men, it starts with the soft voice that speaks to our deepest fear: That we aren't man enough.

pornography

a pornographic world

[WHAT IS NORMAL?]

MY STORY

I am a normal guy in a world in which no guy is really normal. I was raised in a conventional household (two parents, three siblings, one dog) in a part of the United States not known for radical thinking or countercultural lifestyles (Fargo, North Dakota). There I was exposed to the standard US ideology of male dominance, white supremacy, the inherent superiority of capitalism, and America's role as the moral exemplar of the world. I was raised to be a nice white guy who took his place in the world, worked hard, and didn't complain too much.

At the same time, there are aspects of my biography that are not so normal, such as experiences of abuse early in my life. But it turns out, when you start talking to guys, such things happened to lots of us. My sexual profile also might, at first glance, seem outside the norm; I have had sexual relationships with men and women, though most of my life has been lived as a heterosexual. But it turns out that such sexual ambiguity isn't so unusual for lots of men either.

As a child growing up, until my late teens, I typically was the shortest boy in my class and painfully thin. As a small, "faggy" kid, I knew I was an easy target. So, I spent a lot of energy trying not to appear to be homosexual. And it turns out that a lot of the men of my generation whom I have talked to over the years—no matter how macho they appeared on the surface—worried at some point about being tagged as gay when they were young.

Even with my lack of physical ability, I managed to be minimally competent in sports and played on baseball and basketball teams through junior high. Emotionally, I was what's typically called a "sensitive child," but I managed to fake my way through the routine interactions with other boys without getting beaten up. Other boys were not so lucky. I remember one in particular in junior high who endured endless cruelty for being a gangly, socially awkward kid. When other boys teased and attacked him, I stepped aside. I didn't actively participate in that abuse, but I never defended the boy; my fear of being similarly targeted kept me silent. As I write this, 35 years later, I can recall how deeply I empathized with his suffering, and how terrified I was of those boys turning on me.

I have never felt like a "real man," but it turns out that almost no man I know feels much confidence in that realm; even those who fit the specifications more closely rarely feel like they are fulfilling their masculine obligations. So, I wasn't normal, and at the same time I was well within the norm. Most important, I was raised to be normal. I was socialized to be a man, even if I lacked some of the physical or emotional attributes to fill the role very well. And part of that socialization involved the use of pornography.

PORNOGRAPHY USE

I was born in 1958, in the post-*Playboy* world. My first recollection of viewing sexual material is from early grade school, when one of the boys in my school got his hands on a biker magazine that had pictures of women with exposed breasts. I have no recollection of the specific images but do retain a clear memory of gathering in the backyard of a neighborhood boy's house to look at the magazine, which we had hidden under a leaf pile. It was at about the same time I began "playing doctor," exploring bodies with other boys and girls in the neighborhood. So, as I was consciously becoming aware of sexuality, my first recognizable cultural lesson on the subject came in a male-bonding ritual around men's use of an objectified woman, who existed only to provide sexual excitement for us.

[A footnote: This memory is so powerful that every time I see a poster called "Celebrate the Whole Boy" I am reminded of it. The picture on the poster is of five grade-school boys after football practice in the park as they listen to one of the boys playing the violin. In the picture it is fall, with leaves on the ground. Three of the boys are kneeling around the violin case, with the other two standing. The obvious irony is that a poster with a healthy message—that the culture's narrow conception of masculinity limits boys' development and that we should think of all the ways to nurture them—reminds me of the patriarchal training it is critiquing.]

That grade-school experience is the first recollection I have of what Sheila Jeffreys calls "the idea of prostitution," the notion that men can buy women's sexuality in various forms. Rather than seeing men's control and use of women for sex as natural and stemming from a biological imperative, Jeffreys argues that such behavior is socially constructed. "The idea of prostitution has to exist in a man's head first if he is to consider using a woman that way," she writes. "A necessary component of this idea is that it will be sexually exciting to so use a woman."[1]

So, let's mark my introduction into the idea of prostitution at age seven, gathered around the leaf pile, one of a group of boys experiencing our emerging sexuality in an act of male dominance, the ideological assertion of dominance made into a material reality in a picture. That magazine would decay by winter but, in those few months of fall, it taught us something about what it meant to be a man.

The story goes downhill from there.

In the 1960s and 70s, as I went through public school, the main medium for pornography was the magazine, and in my circle of friends there was a reasonably steady supply of them, tucked away under beds, shoved in the back of closets, and carefully hidden under piles of leaves. Some were pilfered from relatives—we all knew where dads and big brothers hid their stash. Others were retrieved from dumpsters; we knew when stores that sold pornography threw away out-of-date stock. Sometimes we looked at them in groups, sometimes alone.

At the end of junior high school and my first year of high school, I was hanging out with a group of guys who had learned the art of sneaking into movie theaters without paying. One of our targets was the Broadway Theater in Fargo, my hometown's only "dirty movie theater," where I saw parts of several hard-core pornographic films as a teenager. At the time I had no sexual experience beyond a few sessions of sexual experimentation with other kids (boys and girls) in grade school, and I really didn't understand much of what was happening on the screen, though I was transfixed by the intensity of my sexual reaction. At a conventional movie theater we sneaked in to see *Last Tango in Paris*, to which I had the same reaction and of which I understood even less.

[Another footnote: In one of those episodes at the Broadway, three of us approached the rear door in the alley with the intention of sneaking in. At the last minute, one of the other boys backed out, claiming to be nervous. But he encouraged us to go ahead, which we did. Once in the theater, we were extremely nervous, desperately afraid of being caught. A few minutes into the film, my companion thought he heard an usher coming toward us and decided to bolt for the exit, with me a few steps behind. He hit the exit door at full speed and met some resistance, but pushed it open and tumbled into the alley, falling over garbage cans. The friend who had stayed behind had dragged the cans in front of the door, assuming that when we tried to exit, we would find it blocked and get scared. Although we were angry at him in the moment, it never occurred to me that such a prank was quite a strange thing to do to a friend. Such cruelty was simply part of growing up male.]

In college, after becoming legally able to enter adult bookstores and theaters, I made occasional visits. Because there was only one such bookstore in Fargo and we risked being seen by friends or relatives while entering or leaving (not to mention while inside), most of those forays took place during trips to Minneapolis, again sometimes with friends and sometimes alone. While in college I also saw a few X-rated movies with friends (both all-male and mixed-gender groups), who treated the outings as campy fun, and I went to a couple of those movies on my own.

[One last footnote: One of my friends from college with whom I made a couple of those trips was a man with whom I had a sexual experience after we had graduated. He was among the most militantly heterosexual men I have ever known and, to the best of my knowledge, did not have a secret gay life. That experience is a reminder that the way most men present themselves to the world in sexual terms does not reflect the complexity of our lives, and we rarely have places to talk openly about that experience. It's one of the most obvious ways in which heterosexism/homophobia limits all men.]

In my 20s, as a working professional, I had a complex relationship to pornography. I typically did not purchase pornography to use at home, although through the years I occasionally bought magazines such as *Playboy* and *Penthouse*. I never showed pornography to women with whom I was involved, with the exception of one trip to an adult theater with a woman in college. I have never made homemade pornography or recorded sexual activity.

Throughout my 20s I would sometimes visit the stores or theaters, though I was increasingly uncomfortable using the material. I had no political critique at that point, nor did I have moral qualms about it; I was then, and remain today, a secular person and had no theological conflicts about the subject. My hesitations were emotional—it just felt wrong. I fell into what I later learned was a common pattern: I would feel intense sexual excitement, masturbate, and immediately feel a sense of shame. That experience would typically lead to a decision to stop using pornography, which would last for some weeks or months. But eventually I would find myself back in a bookstore or theater.

PORNOGRAPHIC FALLOUT

That pattern continued until I was about 30 years old, when I started graduate school and began studying the feminist critique of pornography. Since then, I have used pornography only in the course of four research projects on the content of video and internet pornography.

When people ask me the last time I used pornography—not as a researcher but as a consumer—my answer is "yesterday." By that, I don't mean that I watched a pornographic film yesterday, but that for those of us with a history of "normal" pornography use as children and young adults, quitting pornography doesn't necessarily mean we are pornography-free. My sexual imagination was in part shaped by the use of pornography. I still have in my head vivid recollections of specific scenes in pornographic films I saw 25 years ago. To the degree possible, I try to eliminate those images when I am engaging in sexual activity today (whether alone or with my partner), and I think I'm pretty successful at it. The longer I'm away from pornography, the easier it gets. But the key term is "to the degree possible."

Even with the advances in neuroscience, we really don't know all that much about human memory, consciousness, and behavior. What is pretty clear is that what goes on in our heads and bodies is far more complex than we can ever fully understand. It would not be surprising if the images and ideas that we encounter during the act of achieving orgasm—especially early in our development—would have a powerful influence on us, one that might last in various ways throughout our lives.

What goes on in my body sexually is the result of not just what I think and feel in the moment, but a lifetime of training and experience. I wish I could neatly segregate and eliminate not only the effects of my past pornography use but the effects of all the ugly sexist training I have received in my life about sexuality. I wish I could wall myself off from the sexist messages and images that are all around me today. I wish I could find a way to create a space untouched by those forces in which I could live.

But if I am to be honest, I have to admit something that is painful to face: I still struggle against those forces. I have to work to bracket out of my mind—to the degree possible—those images. I have to work to remember that I can deepen my own experience of intimacy and sexuality only when I let go of those years of training in how to dominate.

It's hard to be honest about these things, because so much of what lives within us is rooted in that domination/subordination dynamic. But it's a good rule of thumb that the things that are difficult are the most important to confront. That's easy to say but hard to practice.

THE CULTURE'S STORY

When I was born in 1958, the cultural conversation on pornography took place largely within a framework of moral assertions. The obscenity law that regulated sexual material was typically defended as necessary because such uses of sex were immoral, while defenders of pornography argued that individuals should be free to use such material because there was no harm to others and the state should not make moral decisions for people. The anti-pornography view was articulated mostly by conservative and religious people; liberals and secular people dominated the defense of pornography.

Beginning in the late 1970s, feminist anti-violence activists began to focus on the connections between men's violence against women and mass media, especially pornography. The framework for that critique was political; feminists were not arguing that any particular expression of sexuality was immoral. Instead, they focused on the political—on differences in power and men's subordination of women, and the concrete harms that followed.

By the mid-1990s, the feminist critique of pornography mostly had been pushed out of the public discussion and a new economic framework emerged. Journalists began writing routinely about pornography as an ordinary business that raised no particular moral or political concerns. These stories sometimes mentioned opposition to the industry, but simply as one aspect of doing business that pornographers had to cope with. Neither the conservative/religious objections to pornography[2] nor the feminist critique[3] has disappeared, but the shift in the framework—the predominant way in which the culture engages pornography—is revealing. Opposition to pornography in the United States, rooted either in conservative religious faith or feminist politics, must articulate that position in a society that largely takes pornography as an uncontroversial part of contemporary culture. This is the normalization or mainstreaming of pornography.

I had been observing that normalization trend for two decades when I went for the first time, in January 2005, to the Adult Entertainment Expo sponsored by *Adult Video News*, the preeminent trade magazine of the pornography industry. Although I had been studying the industry for years, I had always avoided going to the AVN convention, which is held in Las Vegas. When I went in 2005 as part of the crew for a documentary on the industry, I finally understood why I had always instinctively stayed away.

LAS VEGAS

My job at the AEE was to move around on the convention floor with the film's director, Miguel Picker, and talk to the pornography producers, performers, and fans about why they make, distribute, and consume sexually explicit media. As we roamed the huge Sands Expo and Convention Center, which accommodated about 300 booths and thousands of people a day, rock music pulsated from multiple directions. There were photos of naked women everywhere, video screens running porn loops scattered throughout the hall, display tables of dildos and sex dolls. And around every corner were performers in various states of undress, signing posters and posing for pictures. Flashes popped constantly as fans photographed their favorite stars.

At the end of the first day of shooting, Miguel and I were tired. We had spent the day surrounded by images of women being presented and penetrated for the sexual pleasure of men. I had listened to young men tell me that pornography had taught them a lot about what women really want sexually. I had listened to a pornography producer tell me that he thinks anal sex is popular in pornography because men like to think about fucking their wives and girlfriends in the ass to pay them back for being bitchy. And I interviewed the producer who takes great pride that his Gag Factor series was the first to feature exclusively aggressive "throat fucking."

We walked silently from the convention center to the hotel, until I finally said, "I need a drink."

I don't want to feign naïveté. I wasn't particularly shocked by anything I saw that day. There was no one thing I learned on the convention floor that surprised me, nothing anyone said that was really that new to me. I had been working on the issue for more than 15 years at that point; it would have been hard for me to find anything at AEE shocking.

We stopped at the nearest hotel bar (which didn't take long, given how many bars there are in a Las Vegas hotel). I sat down with a glass of wine, and Miguel and I started to talk, searching for some way to articulate what we had just experienced, what we felt. I struggled to hold back tears, and then finally stopped struggling.

I hadn't had some sort of epiphany about the meaning of pornography. It's just that in that moment, the reality of the industry—of the products the industry creates and the way in which they are used—all came crashing down on me. My defenses were inadequate to combat a simple fact: The pornographers had won. The feminist arguments about justice and the harms of pornography had lost. The pornographers not only are thriving, but are more mainstream and normalized than ever. They can fill up a Las Vegas convention center, with the dominant culture paying no more notice than it would to the annual boat show.

My tears at that moment were for myself, because I realized in a more visceral way than ever that the pornographers had won and are helping to construct a world that is not only dangerous for women and children, but also one in which I have fewer and fewer places to turn as a man. Fewer places to walk and talk and breathe that haven't been colonized and pornographized. As I sat there, all I could say to Miguel was, "I don't want to live in this world."

I think Miguel didn't quite know what to make of my reaction. He was nice to me, but he must have thought I was going a bit over the top. I don't blame him; I was a bit over the top. After all, we were there to make a documentary film about the industry, not live out a melodrama about my angst in a Las Vegas hotel bar. The next day Miguel and I hit the convention floor again. At the end of that day, as we walked away, I made the same request. We sat at the same bar. I had another glass of wine and cried again. I think Miguel was glad it was the last day. So was I.

Two days after we left Las Vegas, Miguel called me from New York. This time he was the one crying. He told me that he had just come to his editing studio and had put on some music that he finds particularly beautiful, and then the floodgates opened. "I understand what you meant in the bar," he said, speaking through his own tears.

I tell this story not to highlight the sensitivity of two new-age men. Miguel actually is a sensitive person, though not very new age. I'm not new age, and I don't feel particularly sensitive these days. I often feel harsh and angry. Instead, I tell the story to remind myself that I am alive, that I haven't given up, that I still feel.

I tell the story to remind myself that I'm not alone in that struggle. In a world that trains men to struggle with each other for dominance and keep their emotional distance from each other, Miguel and I could connect. He's a musician and artist from Chile; I'm a journalist and professor from North Dakota. On the surface, we don't have much in common, except our humanity.

I have to remind myself of those things because in the short term, things are grim. The feminist critique that could help this culture transcend its current crisis—on every level, from the intimate to the global—has been attacked and marginalized, and the feminists with the courage to take the critique to the public have been demonized and insulted. That's the short term. In the long term, I believe human society will move out of patriarchy and into some other organizing principle that will emerge through struggle. The problem is, as the economist John Maynard Keynes put it, in the long run we're all dead.

Hope in the long run is rational only when we are willing to face difficult analyses and action in the short term.

ANALYZING PORNOGRAPHY

One of the problems in generating an honest discussion about pornography is that it is often treated as a unique phenomenon. Many conservatives see pornography as intrinsically immoral, while many liberals defend it without evaluating it. Because the content is sexually explicit, people often abandon basic guidelines they would follow if trying to understand another mass media form. For example, I recently had an e-mail exchange with a liberal writer working on a book on pornography, and she suggested that one of the films I had analyzed in a magazine piece—*Gag Factor #10*—was considerably different than the ones she was considering. "I would be happy to give you a list of films I've found interesting," she wrote.

In the context of our exchange, I took the implication of her comment to be that because the Gag Factor series is harsh and overtly misogynist, it was somehow unfair of me to focus on it in my article. I wrote back, pointing out that I was conducting research on the pornography that consumers used most frequently.

My response:

> You can rent any of hundreds of similar titles and find exactly the same content. It's the dominant part of the market. When I study films, I am looking not for what I find interesting, but for what is most commonly rented and purchased. I look at the "mainstream" of the industry, to find out what the majority of men are watching.

I never heard back from her.

My point was simple: The pornographers released 13,588 new films in the previous year. I am sure that out of those I could find a handful of films that were "interesting" to me. A thoughtful meditation on a small number of interesting films might be of value. Of more pressing concern, however, is the large number of films watched by men whose main criteria is not "interesting" but "sex acts on the screen that will arouse me most efficiently and allow me to masturbate to orgasm in a pleasurable fashion." It might be easier or more comforting to pretend that the pornography industry isn't churning out thousands of overtly misogynistic films each year. But it's not clear why we would want to ignore that reality if we are trying to understand the real world.

We should approach the study of pornography as we would any product of the mass media—by studying what messages it contains, how it is produced, and how it is used by people in everyday life. In the terminology of mass communication research, that means looking at:

> » Textual analysis—what are the codes and conventions of the genre, what narrative strategies are used, and what ideology is conveyed by the product?

> » Political economy—how is the production of the product organized, what are the conditions under which it is produced, how is it financed, and who profits?

> » Reception studies—how do people actually use the product, under what conditions do they consume it, what role does it play in their lives?

In this book, I will focus on the first of these analyses, the content of contemporary mass-marketed heterosexual pornography. I will address important political and ethical questions that arise in the study of the pornography industry and how consumers use pornography, but my focus will be on the material itself.

In addition, it is crucial to remember that mass media products don't exist in a vacuum; we have to study them in the real-world social context in which they are produced and used. That is, we have to keep an eye on what is going on in the culture in which all these words and images are circulating. In the contemporary United States, that means recognizing that we live in a rape culture.

I want to return here to radical feminism. In its analysis of the patriarchal system in which we live, a key site of men's oppression of women—a key method of control and domination—is sexuality. In the words of feminist philosopher Marilyn Frye:

> For females to be subordinated and subjugated to males on a global scale … billions of female individuals, virtually all who see life on this planet, must be reduced to a more-or-less willing toleration of subordination and servitude to men. The primary sites of this reduction are the sites of heterosexual relation and encounter—courtship and marriage-arrangement, romance, sexual liaisons, fucking, marriage, prostitution, the normative family, incest and child sexual assault. It is on this terrain of heterosexual connection that girls and women are habituated to abuse, insult, degradation, that girls are reduced to women—to wives, to whores, to mistresses, to sex slaves, to clerical workers and textile workers, to the mothers of men's children.[4]

That is not to suggest that every man treats every woman as a sex slave. Rather, it is to suggest that in this patriarchy in which we live, men generally are trained through a variety of cultural institutions to view sex as the acquisition of pleasure by the taking of women. Men are trained to see sex as a sphere in which they are naturally dominant and women are naturally passive. Women are objectified and women's sexuality is commodified. Sex is sexy because men are dominant and women are subordinate; power is eroticized.

The predictable result of this state of affairs is a world in which violence, sexualized violence, sexual violence, and violence-by-sex is so common that it must be considered to be normal—that is, an expression of the sexual norms of the culture, not violations of the norms. That doesn't mean the culture openly endorses rape, but it does endorse a vision of masculinity that makes rape inviting.

The result is a world in which more than half of college women interviewed in one study reported being victims of some level of sexual aggression. More disturbing, only 27 percent of women whose experience met the legal definition of rape labeled themselves as rape victims. And perhaps even more disturbing, 47 percent of the men who had committed rape said they expected to engage in a similar assault in the future, and 88 percent of men who reported having committed an assault that met the legal definition of rape were adamant that they had not committed rape.[5] We live in a culture in which the sex-domination nexus is so tight that victim and victimizer alike often do not recognize the violence in acts that the society has deemed violent enough to be illegal. That's a rape culture.

For more than two decades, feminists have quoted the statistic that one of three girls is sexually abused in this country. That figure comes from an early 1980s study of 930 women in San Francisco, in which 38 percent of the women reported that they had been sexually abused before age 18.[6] Since then, researchers in Toronto found that of the 420 women they interviewed, 54 percent had been sexually abused before age 16.[7] Just exactly how much rape and child sexual assault is there in this culture? Given the pressure on women and children not to talk about sexual abuse, we aren't likely to ever know. But we do know that the number is so high that the fictions that in this world men put women up on a pedestal, or that women use sex to control men, must be replaced with a painful truth:

We live in a world that hates women and children.[8]

That is a harsh statement, and one that many men and women would reject. When I have made that statement in public talks, men typically strenuously object. "I don't hate women, I love them. I'm married to a woman I love, and I love my children," they say. Women often defend the men in their lives, saying they feel loved by them.

By asserting that this is a woman-hating world, I am not suggesting that every man hates every woman. Nor am I saying that all men engage in overtly misogynistic behavior. When we talk about trends in a society, we are trying to understand patterns, and to identify a pattern in human affairs is not to assert that every single person behaves the same way. But that individual variation does not mean we cannot identify patterns and learn from them.

I learned that men hate women, and I was trained to hate women, in the locker room. Not just in actual gym locker rooms, but in all-male spaces, in those places where men are alone with each other and talk with the knowledge no women will hear them. Men almost never talk in public about what they say in locker rooms, and women—by definition—are not there to hear it. In those spaces, men talk about how they really feel, or think they are supposed to feel, about women. It is very often a language of contempt, of frank discussion about what women are really good for.

We can all see how men hate women and children by a simple observation: No society would let happen what happens to women and children in this culture if at some level it did not have contempt for them. We allow women and children to be raped at a rate that can lead to no other conclusion except that we place a lesser value on their lives.

Men have a stake in believing that we are not really like that. Women have a stake in believing men really don't see them that way. For each party, facing the truth often feels as if it is too much to bear. So we turn away and pretend.

And that's why this culture is so afraid of pornography. The woman-hating in pornography is right there, on the surface, fixed forever onto the printed page, the film stock, the videotape, the DVD, the computer chip. Pornography is a mirror of the way this culture hates women and children, which is why it is important that we look at it, honestly.

pornography as mirror
[CONTENT]

DEFINITIONS

R eaders may have noticed that we are a quarter of the way
into a book about pornography that has yet to define the
term. Given the long-standing debates over the issue of how to
define pornography—or, for some, whether it can be defined—
that may seem a shortcoming. But the strategy of delayed definition is quite conscious, for two reasons. First, readers likely
have been able to follow all the arguments so far, even if the
category is not precisely defined in a way that allows us to cat-
egorize every sexual image in the world as pornography or not
pornography. In contemporary US culture there is a coherent-
enough shared sense of the meaning of the term that allows
conversation to go forward. Second, too often people use what
I have called the "definitional dodge" to avoid confronting the
core issues that pornography raises. The dodge usually involves
some combination of:

» It's all a matter of taste.

» What is pornography to some is erotica to
others.

» What is degrading to some is liberating to
others.

» There's no way to talk about sexually explicit
material that doesn't eventually collapse into
subjective judgments.

» We cannot define the term with precision, so therefore we cannot say much of anything about pornography.

As D. H. Lawrence put it, "What is pornography to one man is the laughter of genius to another."[1]

In my experience, this retreat behind the definitional dodge is either a cynical attempt by pro-pornography forces to cut off critique before it can be voiced, or a fear-driven response by people who are unsure that they want to go where an honest confrontation with pornography will take us. Better, from those points of view, to stay stuck arguing about definitions. But there are many terms we use routinely that cannot be defined precisely. Why is a sport utility vehicle more appropriately designated a "light truck" instead of a "passenger car"? What makes one dish on the menu an "appetizer" and another an "entrée"? When does a "news story" that overtly includes the writer's opinion become an "analysis piece," which is different from an "editorial"? The words we use to mark categories come in varying degrees of precision, and the lack of absolute clarity in the meaning of words does not render words useless. In many situations, we understand that politics and/or profit motive affect how words are defined.

We don't need what lawyers call "bright-line rules" to begin a discussion. We can recognize that it is through discussion that we refine our understanding of the categories. In fact, when definitions for a particular debate are difficult to nail down, that's precisely when we need a collective conversation and should avoid collapsing into individual judgments; we deepen our understanding through conversation.

In the legal arena—deciding whether and/or how we should deal with sexually explicit material through the law—the issue of definitions may seem more important, but concerns about legal terms need not derail a wider conversation in the culture. When one isn't arguing about law, arguments about legal definitions aren't relevant. Remember also that pornography is not necessarily more difficult to define legally than any other term. One of the things that law does is create definitions through application and use. And the struggle over definitions is a political as well as legal battle, one that takes place both inside and outside the legal arena.[2]

In the context of the necessary conversation, I suggest that we let the market define the category: Pornography is the material sold in pornography shops and on pornography websites, for the purpose of producing sexual arousal for the mostly male consumers. I recognize this does not define the term with absolute precision, but it's sufficiently clear to make conversation possible. When men want pornography, they know where to go. So, let's follow the guys, follow the money. This doesn't mean that every single item in a pornography shop is pornography, or that pornography isn't sold in other places. But let's start with what the culture uses as a working definition—the graphic sexually explicit material sold for the purpose of arousing and satisfying sexual desire.

From a feminist point of view, we also can talk about pornography as a specific kind of sexual material that helps maintain the sexual subordination of women. In Andrea Dworkin's words:

> In the subordination of women, inequality itself is sexualized: made into the experience of sexual pleasure, essential to sexual desire. Pornography is the material means of sexualizing inequality; and that is why pornography is a central practice in the subordination of women.[3]

Dworkin gives us a way to think about what we might call "the elements of the pornographic," the ways in which that subordination is enacted. Not all pornography includes all these elements, but all these elements are present throughout contemporary pornography:

» Objectification: when "a human being, through social means, is made less than human, turned into a thing or commodity, bought and sold."

» Hierarchy: a question of power, with "a group on top (men) and a group on the bottom (women)."

» Submission: when acts of obedience and compliance become necessary for survival, members of oppressed groups learn to anticipate the orders and desires of those who have power over

[handwritten marginal notes: "Just true of women! Also true of men of color, homosexuals, children in porn, times in porn, in other ways — More about the power than the person"]

them, and their compliance is then used by the dominant group to justify its dominance.

» Violence: when it becomes "systematic, endemic enough to be unremarkable and normative, usually taken as an implicit right of the one committing the violence."[4]

So, the task is to analyze pornography (in the first sense, as a description of a type of material easily identifiable in the market) to determine if it is pornographic (in the feminist sense, as an expression of male-supremacist sexual ideology).

Before examining that, a bit more on categories: This chapter will concern itself only with the mass-marketed heterosexual pornography that is readily available in the United States, focusing on movies. By "heterosexual," I mean those videotapes and DVDs depicting primarily heterosexual sexual activity that are most commonly used by the predominantly heterosexual male clientele. In these films there often are "girl/girl" sex scenes that follow the conventions of heterosexual porn sex, typically involving penetration with dildos and other sex toys. There are also gay and lesbian pornography genres, which are of interest for many reasons. But, while there are no completely reliable figures available, it's clear that the bulk of the market is heterosexual pornography. I focus on that segment of the market in part because it is the obvious place to examine the core patriarchal ideology of pornography, and in part because of the potential effects on male sexual behavior.

Within that category, one can find what seem like endless sub-genres of varying levels of explicitness, from soft-core to alleged snuff films.[5] The analysis in this book is based not on the fringes of the market but on the mainstream—those movies that are most commonly rented and purchased. Beginning in 1996, I have conducted three qualitative studies of this material.[6] I focused on movies on VHS and DVD because that medium has eclipsed magazines as the dominant segment of the market. Internet pornography now challenges the DVD, and the openness of the internet does allow for a wider variety of material from a larger number of producers. But it is not yet clear that the content of internet pornography is dramatically different from what is available on DVD.

A second key point: In each study, I looked at 15 movies that were chosen from the shelves of pornography stores in a mid-size (Austin, Texas) or large (Boston, Massachusetts) US city. In each case, the titles were selected by consulting with the store manager and clerks to determine the most popular movies in a representative sample of categories. I did not select movies from the sadomasochism or bondage categories, or from fringe sub-genres such as urination or defecation movies. Feminist critics of pornography are often accused of selecting the most violent and degrading movies to analyze and then pretending such movies are representative of the industry. I wanted to make sure such a criticism could not be made of this work.

In addition to those systematic studies, I have watched another set of films in my role as a consultant to a larger quantitative study of pornography conducted by a research team in 2005–06. That study randomly selected 50 movies from a list of the top 250 rented VHS and DVD pornographic movies from December 2004 to June 2005. My viewing in that project was less systematic; I watched parts of many films and 10 in their entirety. I intended to view 15 films, as in my previous studies, but found that what I was learning from continued viewing was not worth the emotional cost to me. In short, I had seen enough and had reached a saturation point—watching additional films was not adding to my understanding, but it was taking a toll on my psyche (more on that later). It was time for me to exit the pornographic world. But in that decade, I spent more than adequate time in that world to describe it.

AN OVERVIEW

The pornography industry produces two major styles of films, "features" (the two most well-known feature production companies are Vivid and Wicked) and "gonzo" (produced by many companies, including Evil Angel, Anabolic, and Red Light District). Pornographic features mimic, however badly, the conventions of a Hollywood movie. There is some minimal plot, character development, and dialogue, all in the service of presenting the explicit sex. Gonzo films have no such pretensions; they are simply recorded sex, often in a private home or on some minimal set. These films often start with an interview with the woman or women about their sexual desires before the man or men enter the scene. The industry's dominant trade magazine, *Adult Video News*, uses two terms for these no-plot movies:

» Wall-to-wall: "All-sex productions without plot structures. A series of sex scenes that may or may not include a connecting device."

» Gonzo: "Porno verite or reality-based porn, in which performers acknowledge the presence of the camera, frequently addressing viewers directly through it."

In everyday discussion, both among producers and consumers, it appears that the finer points of this distinction evaporate, and the pornography world is divided between features and gonzo.

Pornographic films are also sometimes categorized by a hard-core/soft-core distinction. Soft-core films, typically seen on cable television channels such as Cinemax, include nudity, sexual petting, and intercourse presented without the display of genitals or penetration. Hard-core films—available in shops, through mail order, or on the internet—include virtually any sexual activity imaginable, in graphic detail, with close-up shots of genitals and penetration.

All these films use performers who are 18 or over. Child pornography—sexually explicit material using minors, which is the only type of pornography that is without a doubt illegal everywhere in the United States—is available but only underground or through computer networks. Pornographic movies that focus on cheerleaders, babysitters, and other categories of girls and young women—what might be called pseudo-child pornography—attempt to create the idea of sex with minors. But ever since the 1980s scandal involving Traci Lords, who performed illegally in hard-core movies when she was a teenager, the industry has been especially careful not to use minors.

Whether analyzing feature or gonzo movies, a few basic themes are common to all mass-marketed heterosexual pornography:

» all women at all times want sex from all men;

» women like all the sexual acts that men perform or demand; and

» any woman who does not at first realize this can be easily turned with a little force. Such force is rarely necessary, however, for most of the women in pornography are the "nymphomaniacs" that men fantasize about.

The message of pornography is not just that women choose this kind of sex, but that it is their nature, a part of being a woman. For example, the text of a banner for the website suckmebitch.com, which promises "raw & uncut real home blowjob videos," expresses this succinctly: "Make her feel like a real woman. Just say the magic words … Suck Me Bitch."

In the pornographic world, a female person becomes a woman—a real woman—by taking her role as a "Dirty Little Cock Sucker." Feminist legal scholar and activist Margaret Baldwin sums it up accurately:

> In pornography, the world is a balanced and harmonious place. The sexual requirements of women and men are perfectly congruent, symbiotic in relation and polar in definition: women live to be fucked, men inevitably fuck.[7]

It really is that simple because pornography is that formulaic. Whatever the level of plot and character development, the focus is on the sexual acts, and those acts proceed in predictable fashion. In the more sedate features, a short period of the man performing oral sex on the woman is followed by a longer period of her performing oral sex on him, followed by vaginal penetration in a variety of positions. In some features, vaginal will be followed by anal penetration, before the "cum shot" or "money shot"—the man ejaculating onto the woman's body or into her mouth. The vocalizations in features vary somewhat. Women almost always ask/beg the men to fuck them, often encouraging them to penetrate them harder. The men's performance can vary from relatively benign vocalizations of their pleasure to the more aggressive "take this"/"you know you want it" script.

In gonzo, those same acts are featured but typically are performed in rougher fashion, often with more than one man involved, and with more explicitly denigrating language that marks women as sluts, whores, cunts, nasty bitches, and so on. In gonzo there also is an expanded repertoire of sexual acts, including several distinctive sex practices that are, if not unique to pornography, certainly far more prevalent in pornography than in the world off camera. Those include the double penetration, double anal, double vag, and ass-to-mouth.

Understanding pornography's use of those acts requires discussion of the role of anal sex in pornography. Prior to the late 1980s and 90s, anal sex was not routine in mainstream pornography. As legal constraints on pornography relaxed in the mid-1970s and the normalizing of pornography began, pornographers started to look for ways to make their products edgy, and the first place they went was anal sex. Why anal penetration of women?

Anal sex can be pleasurable for the person being penetrated. Certainly the frequency of the practice among gay men suggests that is the case, and some women also enjoy the practice. But it's also clear that most women do not seek out anal penetration,[8] and therein lies the answer: Pornography, with its overwhelming male clientele, moves toward sexual acts that women in day-to-day life do not seek out because most women find them either not pleasurable, painful, or denigrating. Those are the very same acts that men seem to find intensely pleasurable to watch in pornography. A pornography industry executive explained the appeal of anal sex this way:

> Essentially, it comes from every man who's unhappily married, and he looks at his wife who just nagged at him about this or that or whatnot, and he says, "I'd like to fuck you in the ass." He's angry at her, right? And he can't, so he would rather watch some girl taking it up the ass and fantasize at that point he's doing whatever girl happened to be mean to him that particular day, and that is the attraction, because when people watch anal, nobody wants to watch a girl enjoying anal.[9]

No doubt this executive overstates the case; there are many films in which women appear to enjoy anal penetration, indicating many men enjoy the image of women getting pleasure that way. But it's also true that many films portray women enduring, not enjoying, anal penetration. Sometimes this is made explicit, as in the website AnalSuffering.com, which promises, "Nothing makes these sluts hornier and nastier than the pain caused by a huge cock ramming up their tight asses."

By the late 1990s, anal penetration in heterosexual pornography had become routine—not all movies included it, but it was no longer unusual. The industry looked for other acts that could push the conventional sexual script, without venturing into territory that would bring increased pressure from law enforcement. A widely circulated memo from an industry lawyer, written in 2000 amid fears that the incoming Bush administration would pursue obscenity prosecutions more vigorously than had Clinton officials, listed acts that could land producers in legal trouble,[10] though virtually everything on the list was, and remains, standard practice in the industry.[11]

DOUBLING PATRIARCHAL PLEASURE

There is a wide variety of sexual acts that one can find in pornography, but the ones that became commonplace in gonzo pornography by the early 2000s—and slowly began to find their way into features—include

» double penetration, known as "DP" in the industry, in which a woman is penetrated vaginally and anally at the same time;

» double anal, in which a woman is penetrated anally by two men at the same time;

» double vag, in which a woman is penetrated vaginally by two men at the same time; and

» ass-to-mouth, known as "ATM" in the industry, in which a man removes his penis from a woman's anus and, without cleaning it, places it in her mouth or the mouth of another woman.

I am not a woman, and so I obviously cannot experience a DP or a double vag. I have not experienced a double anal or ATM. So, while I speak without knowing how such acts feel, I think it is uncontroversial to say that the vast majority of women do not seek out such practices in their lives. From watching these acts on screen, it's also reasonable to assume—even though women performers routinely say they enjoy them—that they are hard on a woman's body and require conditioning to endure.

Belladonna, a well-known gonzo pornography performer, in an interview with ABC News described such scenes this way:

> You have to really prepare physically and mentally for it. I mean, I go through a process from the night before. I stop eating at 5:00. I do, you know, like two enemas. The next morning I don't eat anything. It's so draining on your body.[12]

The most plausible explanation of the popularity of these acts is that men know that women in the world outside pornography do not want to engage in such acts and, unless forced, will not participate. Men know that—and they find it sexually arousing to watch them in part because of that knowledge.

Finally, consider ATM. In physical terms, it's difficult to imagine that a man's pleasure is enhanced by a woman taking his penis in her mouth directly from her anus or another woman's anus; that act does not increase the physical stimulation of nerve endings. So, why do it? Again, the most plausible explanation is clear: To suck a man's penis directly from an anus is unhygienic and potentially dangerous. When a woman does it, she is either expressing disregard for her own health or accepting the man's implicit imposition of the idea that her health is of no concern. Either way, she is less than fully human.

Even someone from the industry, writing as the "Anal Advisor" concedes there are health risks in the practice. In response to a letter about the rise of ATM in pornography, she writes:

> Taking your dick out of a woman's ass and directly shoving it into her mouth may make for exciting porn, but, in real life, it can be problematic. Bacteria lives in the butt that may not peacefully exist in the mouth, and could lead to an infection. No matter how squeaky clean her rectum may be, chances are there are at least trace amounts of fecal matter which may end up on your dick—do you really want to make her suck that off? Would you put it in your own mouth?[13]

Even more interesting is the second half of her response, in which she acknowledges the intensity of some men's desire for ATM:

> I have a better idea. Fuck her in the ass til she's right on the edge of orgasm, or you are. Order her to get on her knees and close her eyes. Talk to her, tell her she better open up her mouth for your cock. Have an anti-bacterial baby wipe stashed nearby, and quietly grab it, slide it over your cock, then toss it. Now proceed with sticking your rod in her mouth, keeping the fantasy intact, but keeping it clean for everyone involved.[14]

In other words, it's fine to want to treat a woman as less than fully human and to find sexual pleasure in it, but please do it in a way that is hygienic.

The trends in contemporary pornographic movies are quite clear: The men who consume pornography enjoy watching sexual activity in which women are less than fully human. Men like to watch sexual activity in which women are treated with cruelty. At this point, it's important to describe actual scenes from pornography in some detail. Again, to be clear, what I'm describing is not the fringe of the market but the mainstream of a pornography industry that is increasingly accepted in the mainstream of US society.

GONZO:
"IT WAS TURNING ME ON WHEN I THOUGHT YOU WERE CRYING."

Two scenes from *Two in the Seat #3*, a standard gonzo release from the Red Light District company in 2003:

Claire James says she is 20 years old and has been performing in pornographic films for three months. "I'm here to get pounded," she says, announcing that she would like to perform a double anal that day (the video does not record that act, however). At that point, two men enter the room. One asks, "Are you a dirty, nasty girl? You must be." The other starts to handle her roughly, grabbing her face and slapping her lightly. During the initial round of oral sex, one man holds her head while the other one grabs her pigtails. "All the way down to the balls," one says. During intercourse, the men offer a steady stream of comments such as "You're a little fucking cunt" and "You're such a little slut." At one point, Claire says, "Please put your cock in my ass." During the DP, her vocalizations sound clearly pained. The three are on the floor, with Claire braced against the couch, not moving much. The men spank her, and her buttocks are red. "Yeah, I love it," she says. One man says, "I want to hear you scream." At one point, one of the men asks, "Are you crying?"

> Claire: No, I'm enjoying it.
>
> Man: Damn, I thought you were crying. It was turning me on when I thought you were crying.
>
> Claire: Would you like me to?
>
> Man: Yeah, give me a fucking tear. Oh, there's a fucking tear.

"Feed me your cum," Claire says, displaying the first man's ejaculate in her mouth for the camera. "Swallowed," she says. After the second man' ejaculates, she wipes the semen off her face with her fingers and eats it. The off-camera interviewer asks her how she feels. Claire reports that her asshole feels good: "Feels great. A little raw, but that's good."

In another scene, Jessica Darlin tells the camera she has performed in 200 films and that she's submissive: "I like guys to just take over and just fuck me and have a good time with me. I'm just here for pleasure." The man who enters the room grabs her hair and tells her to beg the other man. She crawls over on her hands and knees, and he spanks her hard. When he grabs her by the throat hard, she seems surprised. The other man comes across the room and grabs her from behind, pulling her hair. During oral sex, he says, "Choke on that dick." She gags. He grabs her head and slaps her face, then forces his penis in her mouth quickly. She gags again. The other man duplicates the action, calling her a "little bitch." Jessica is drooling after gagging; she looks as if she might pass out. The men slap her breasts, and then grab her by the hair and pull her up.

During intercourse, one man grabs her by the throat. At this point, Jessica is moaning/screaming. She sounds, literally, like a wounded animal. The sex continues. One man puts two fingers in her anus and then makes her suck his fingers. She says: "Fuck my ass. I'm a fucking whore. I want you to fuck my ass." The other man spits in her mouth. One man enters her anally from the rear as she is pushed up against the couch. Then the other man enters her anally while his partner puts his foot on her head. One says, "Keep your fucking ass up" when she drops too close to the floor. Finally, one grabs her hair and asks what she wants. "I want you to cum in my mouth," she says. "Give me all that cum. I want to taste it."

FEATURES:
"STICK IT IN MY ASS" AND "DON'T GO ANY DEEPER"

A scene from *Delusional*, a 2000 release from Vivid:

Lindsay, the film's main character, is a woman slow to return to dating after she caught her husband cheating on her. She says she is waiting for the right man—a sensitive man—to come along. Her male coworker, Randy, clearly would like to be that man but must wait as Lindsay explores other sexual experiences, first with a woman named Alex, whom she meets online and assumes is a man. Later, after Alex and Lindsay have sex with a man in the kitchen of a restaurant, Lindsay is finally ready to accept Randy's affection. He takes her home and tells her, "I'll always be here for you no matter what. I just want to look out for you." Lindsay lets down her defenses, and they embrace.

After kissing and removing their clothes, Lindsay begins oral sex on Randy while on her knees on the couch, and he then performs oral sex on her while she lies on the couch. They then have intercourse, with Lindsay saying, "Fuck me, fuck me, please" and "I have two fingers in my ass—do you like that?" This leads to the usual progression of positions: She is on top of him while he sits on the couch, and then he enters her vaginally from behind before he asks, "Do you want me to fuck you in the ass?" She answers in the affirmative. "Stick it in my ass," she says. "I love the way you slide into my asshole. ... Deep in my ass. ... I'm coming on your cock in my ass." After two minutes of anal intercourse, the scene ends with him masturbating and ejaculating on her breasts.

A scene from *Sopornos IV,* a 2003 release from VCA Pictures:

The plot is a takeoff on the popular HBO series about mobsters. Mob boss Bobby Soporno is obsessed with the thought that everyone in his life is always having sex, including his crew and his daughter. The sex between various combinations of these people goes forward in standard feature fashion.

In the final sex scene, Bobby's wife has sex with two of the men in his organization. After oral and vaginal sex, one of the men prepares to penetrate her anally. She tells him: "That fucking cock is so fucking huge. ... Spread [my] fucking ass. ... Spread it open." He penetrates her. Then she says, in a slightly lower tone, "Don't go any deeper," and she seems to be in pain. At the end of the scene, she begs for their semen ("Two cocks jacking off in my face. I want it.") and opens her mouth, and the men ejaculate onto her at the same time.

FEATURES AND GONZO: SIMILARITIES AND DIFFERENCES

When one critiques the blatant misogyny in gonzo, many pornography fans and industry defenders will concede that much of the content is disturbing but will quickly retreat to the idea that features are more egalitarian. There are obvious differences in the type of sexual activity and the level of overt denigration of women, but in both features and gonzo the same three rules apply: All women always want sex from all men, and the sexual acts they want are the ones that men demand, and any woman who doesn't immediately recognize her true sexual nature will understand as soon as sex is forced on her. At the most basic level, contemporary mass-marketed heterosexual pornography—feature or gonzo—is the presentation of the objectified female body for the sexual satisfaction of men.

I use the term "female body" in that sentence instead of "woman" consciously: In pornography, women are not fully human. In pornography, women are three holes and two hands. The essence of a woman is those parts of her body that can produce sexual stimulation in men.

Women are objectified in pornography, many of its defenders will concede, but so are men. Just as women are one-dimensional and obsessively focused on sex in the films, so are men. The defense is that pornography is an equal-opportunity objectifier. While that's true in a superficial sense, it obscures the way in which in pornography women are sexual objects and men are sexual subjects. Sex in pornography is defined by the rise and fall of a man's penis, and during sex his desires almost always determine the direction of the activity. Men have agency and act; women are acted upon.

This is clear in the different ways that oral sex is presented, in both gonzo and features. If there are scenes of men performing cunnilingus, those scenes are much shorter in duration than those of women performing fellatio. When they perform oral sex, men almost always are emotionally mute and unresponsive, while women performing oral sex on men respond as if having a penis in their mouths brings them to orgasm as well as the man. Cunnilingus scenes almost always are set up in such a way as to maximize visibility of the woman's vagina, with men's heads off to the side, rather than directly over the vagina, to make it possible for the camera to see the vagina. Fellatio scenes, on the other hand, are constructed and photographed to center on the female providing pleasure for the man.

The language of pornography also indicates the different status of men and women. Men have penises, but during sex they are not referred to as "penises." Women not only have a vagina but can be reduced to their vagina—a woman is a "cunt." It's not just a part of her body, something she has—it is what she is. Hence the common pornspeak for women: "I am a cunt (or bitch, or whore, or slut). Fuck me with your big cock." She is nothing more than her sexual organ, an object; he remains a subject, one who uses his sexual organ. MacKinnon captures this in her succinct lesson on the grammar of pornography and male dominance: "Man fucks woman; subject verb object."[15]

"INTERRACIAL" RACISM

Contemporary pornography is not only sexist but also racist, in a distinctive manner.

Most people recognize that even with the gains of the civil rights movement in the last half of the 20th century, racism endures in the United States and that the reproduction of that ideology through media is a problem. Race still matters, and media depictions of race matter. In mainstream movies and television, the most blatant and ugly forms of racism have disappeared, although subtler patterns of stereotyping continue. Pornography is the one media genre in which overt racism is still routine and acceptable. Not subtle, coded racism, but old-fashioned US racism—stereotypical representations of the sexually primitive black male stud, the animalistic black woman, the hot Latina, the Asian geisha.

Ironically, the term that the pornography industry uses for the category of overtly racist material is "interracial," which implies cross-racial understanding and cooperation but is something quite different. For example, the director of the Black Attack Gang Bang line of films explains: "My mission is to find the cutest white honeys to get Gang Banged by some hard pipe hitting niggas straight outta Compton!"[16]

The racism of the industry is so pervasive that it goes largely unnoticed. In an interview at the 2005 AEE with Jon B—general manager of Doghouse Digital, the company that produced *Black Bros and Asian Ho's*—I asked if he ever was criticized for the racism of such films. He said, "No, they are very popular." I repeated the question: Popular, yes, but do people ever criticize the racism? He looked incredulous; the question apparently had never entered his mind. He saw no racism in a film that depicted black men as sexually primitive and Asian women as made for sexual servitude.

The interracial category contains most every possible combination of racial groups, with the notable exception of Asian men—they appear rarely in heterosexual pornography but often in gay pornography, where they often are presented as feminine in relation to the masculine white men. But the dominant mode of interracial pornography is black men and white women.

When I interviewed John E. Depth—a black man who performs and directs for his own company, In-Depth Productions—at the 2005 AEE, he said that he didn't really understand why white men like to watch black men having sex with white women in degrading fashion and could only speculate that white men are fascinated with the image of the black man as the "big buck" and are hoping for some thrill from the promised sexual prowess of those men. At the end of the conversation, partly in jest but with some seriousness, he asked rhetorically: "Sometimes I wonder what Martin Luther King would say. We have over-cum?"

The most compelling analysis of this genre comes from Gail Dines, who concludes that interracial pornography of this sort is a kind of "new minstrel show" that functions as a peepshow for whites into what they see as the authentic black life, not on the plantation, but in the "hood" where all the conventions of white civilized society cease to exist. The "hood" in the white racist imagination is a place of pimps, hos and generally uncontrolled black bodies, and the white viewer is invited, for a fee, to slum in this world of debauchery. In the "hood," the white man can dispense with his whiteness by identifying with the black man, and thus can become as sexually skilled and as sexually out-of-control as the black man. Here he does not have to worry about being big enough to satisfy the white woman (or man), nor does he have to concern himself with fears about poor performance or "weak wads" or cages like poor hubby in *Blacks on Blondes* [an interracial film in which the husband is literally in a cage while watching black men have sex with his wife]. Indeed, the "hood" represents liberation from the cage, and the payoff is a satiated white woman (or man) who has been completely and utterly feminized by being well and truly turned into a "fuckee."[17]

Dines points out that the black body that is celebrated as uncontrolled in interracial pornography is the same body that needs to be controlled and disciplined in the real world of white supremacy:

Just as white suburban teenagers love to listen to hip-hop and white adult males gaze longingly at the athletic prowess of black men, the white pornography consumer enjoys his identification with (and from) black males through a safe peephole, in his own home, and in mediated form. The real, breathing, living black man, however, is to be kept as far away as possible from these living rooms, and every major institution in society marshals its forces in the defense of white society. The ideologies that white men take to the pornography text to enhance their sexual pleasure are the very ideologies that they use to legitimize the control of black men: while it may heighten arousal for the white porn user, it makes life intolerable for the real body that is (mis)represented in all forms of white controlled media.[18]

THE CUM SHOT

Feature or gonzo, no matter what color, there's always the cum shot.

The "cum shot" is a nearly universal convention in pornography. For many years the standard shot was of the man ejaculating onto the woman's body. Today, that simple cum shot remains, most often in features, but the industry has developed a wider range of these shots that in gonzo can reach levels so extreme that they seem like self-parody.

Ejaculating outside the body is not, of course, exclusively a pornographic practice. The everyday sexual practices of people can include that act, either for birth-control purposes or because the partners like the warm feel of ejaculate (men and boys certainly know that the feeling can be pleasurable from masturbation). But the pornographic cum shot has developed in ways that clearly do not reflect the practices of the vast majority of people. In gonzo there is an obsession with ejaculating not just on a woman's body but into her mouth, often followed by her blowing bubbles with the semen and letting it flow out of her mouth, and then swallowing it. In scenes with more than one woman, they may pass the semen between them with their hands and/or mouths; this is sometimes called "cum swapping." Other films advertise that the scenes will end with "cum in her eyes." In films that feature a number of men in one scene, a woman can be literally drenched in semen at the end of a scene. The most extreme practice in this genre is called "bukkake," a term that indicates large numbers of men ejaculating onto a woman or women. JM Productions, a gonzo company that advertises its products as being degrading to women, had produced 31 films in the American Bukkake series as of the end of 2006. It advertised a compilation tape, *American Bukkake's Biggest Swallows*, this way:

> This is the movie you've been asking for. We have gone into our vaults and found you the

4 most intense cum swallowing scenes ever filmed. So, if watching girls drink thick chunks of gooey semen is your thing, look no further. Your paradise is their hell. Enjoy.[19]

In the 2001 Wicked release *Infidelity*, the character played by Sydnee Steele is a rock band groupie who says, "I love being covered in cum, the more the better. Now, it's not always pretty, but it sure as hell turns me on." This desire is so strong, she explains, "I'll do whatever they want, and all I ask in return is that they cover me in cum at the end of it all." In this scene, she is penetrated orally and vaginally by three men in various combinations before each man ejaculates on her face or in her mouth. Remember, this film is a feature, different from the coarser gonzo fare. Wicked is one of the two premier producers of features. Sydnee Steele was one of Wicked's top contract performers. This is no underground title; it exemplifies typical mainstream pornography. This is the "top of the line" in pornography.

Some have speculated that the cum shot is a product of the days of silent film, when pornographers needed a way to visually signal the end of sex. But whatever the genesis of the cum shot in the history of pornography,[20] we can ask why it continues. What does the cum shot mean? In one of the first films I watched in my study of pornography, the 1990 release *Taboo VIII*, one of the male characters offers an answer. When this man refuses the request of a woman (whom he feels is a slut) to have intercourse with her, he tells her, "I don't fuck sluts. I jerk off on them. Take it or leave it." He then ejaculates onto her breasts. That suggests that ejaculating onto a woman is a method by which she is turned into a slut, something—not really someone—whose purpose is to be sexual with men. Ejaculating onto her body marks her as a "slut," which in pornography is synonymous with "woman."

That assessment was echoed by a veteran of the pornography industry, who told an interviewer:

> I'd like to really show what I believe the men want to see: violence against women. I firmly believe that we serve a purpose by showing that. The most violent we can get is the cum shot in the face. Men get off behind that, because they

get even with the women they can't have. We try to inundate the world with orgasms in the face.[21]

THE RISE OF GONZO: "WHAT ARE YOU GONNA DO NEXT?"

Features are profitable, but based on my discussions with producers and others in the industry the growth in pornography is in the increasingly harsh gonzo market, whose producers acknowledge that they provide the rougher material that consumers desire. As Jerome Tanner put it during a pornography directors' roundtable discussion featured in *Adult Video News*, "People just want it harder, harder, and harder, because like Ron said, what are you gonna do next?"[22] Another director, Jules Jordan, was blunt about his task:

> One of the things about today's porn and the extreme market, the gonzo market, so many fans want to see so much more extreme stuff that I'm always trying to figure out ways to do something different. But it seems everybody wants to see a girl doing a d.p. now or a gangbang. For certain girls, that's great, and I like to see that for certain people, but a lot of fans are becoming a lot more demanding about wanting to see the more extreme stuff. It's definitely brought porn somewhere, but I don't know where it's headed from there.[23]

Director Mitchell Spinelli, interviewed while filming the first video (*Give Me Gape*[24]) for a series for his new Acid Rain company, seemed clear where it was heading:

> People want more. They want to know how many dicks you can shove up an ass. ... It's like *Fear Factor* meets *Jackass*. Make it more hard, make it more nasty, make it more relentless. The guys make the difference. You need a good guy, who's been around and can give a good scene, fuckin'em hard. I did my homework. These guys are intense.[25]

Here's what "fuckin'em hard" looks like. Two scenes from *A Cum Sucking Whore Named Kimberly*, a 2003 release from Anabolic Video Productions:

The tape is a compilation of five scenes featuring Kimberly, taken from five other films produced by this company. The first scene is from *World Sex Tour #25*, in which two men explain that this will be Kimberly's first anal scene and first DP. One man says, "That asshole is never going to bounce back. But it was fucking romantic as hell. And she swallowed, too. She did the retch and recover."

Kimberly is French Canadian and appears to speak little or no English. The two men run through the standard progression of oral, vaginal, and anal intercourse. The vaginal intercourse is particularly rough, even for a gonzo film. During the anal intercourse the men ease up on the pounding, perhaps out of a recognition that Kimberly can't take that rough of a level of penetration. During the DP she looks frightened and appears to try to speak but is unable to.

At the end of the scene, when the men ejaculate into her mouth, she starts to gag, and the two men tell her (through a translator off-screen) that she has to swallow the semen, which she does. Through the translator, they tell Kimberly to say, "Thank you for fucking me in Montreal." Kimberly says, "Thank you for fucking me in Montreal." The scene ends with the two men talking later about the experience. "We blew out her asshole," one says.

The last scene from the tape is from *Gang Bang Girl #32*, in which a frustrated football coach berates his players on the field after practice, asking them whether they are "football players or fags." He says they will lose the game the next day, which he wouldn't mind if his players were men—he just hates to lose with fags. He turns to the assistant coach and says, "Prove to me they're not fags," before walking away.

The proof comes in the form of 13 players having sex with Kimberly, one of the cheerleaders in the stands. She comes down to the field and engages in sex in a variety of different positions. As the men wait for their turn, they stand around her, masturbating to keep their erections, joking and laughing. At one point she is in a double penetration with a third man's penis in her mouth. In the industry, this is known as "airtight"—all the woman's holes are plugged. During this part of the scene, she also masturbates two other penises. She is three holes and two hands.

One by one the men ejaculate, most of them into Kimberly's mouth. One man ejaculates into a protective cup and then pours it into her mouth. The last man ejaculates inside her vagina, and then she stands and catches his semen in her hand. She moves forward to face the camera and starts to lick it off her hand. At first she can't quite bring herself to do it, but then she does, making a pained face and gagging slightly. The scene ends with the men dumping the water from a large jug on her.

A *Cum Sucking Whore Named Kimberly* is a disturbing movie for the way it reduces this woman to something less than human. But it is hardly the most disturbing movie one can find on the shelves in a pornography store or on the internet.

PORNOGRAPHY'S BAD BOYS

In the industry there are certain producers whose films are so overtly misogynistic that they make other pornographers nervous. These performers and/or directors, who push too far in the eyes of other producers, present a problem for the industry. On the one hand, their material is seen as so extreme that it could bring increased law-enforcement attention to the industry, but at the same time their fellow pornographers reflexively defend almost any sexual material. One of the most controversial in the 1990s and 2000s has been Max Hardcore, known for films in which he not only has rough sex with young-looking women but specializes in, well, it's difficult to explain. Here's how his website puts it:

> Max fucks chicks he finds the way you like to—getting cute cunts on his couch. Using their tight holes to pleasure his stiff cock. Max turns ordinary teens and [mothers] alike into piss and cum-splattered sluts before your eyes.
>
> Max wastes no time, gagging girls on his cock and pissing down their throats before he even learns their email addresses! Max is the originator of rectal-boring action—gaping assholes, and fisting cunts.
>
> Max also uses speculums to pry-open their fuck-holes so you can look deep inside. He'll spray his cum and piss into the gaping tunnels, even making them drink it out of their ass! Whether

[it's a] naïve teen or classy broad, Max delivers the same ruthless treatment.[26]

Some pornography presents women enjoying sex acts that appear to be painful. Other pornography presents women in those situations appearing to be in pain without making any mention of it. Max Hardcore revels in presenting women in pain. In his 2000 release *Max Extreme, Vol. 12*, he explains to Julianna (who is dressed as a schoolgirl but looks to be in her mid to late 20s) that she is a bad girl, and bad girls get "cunt fucked and ass fucked and throat fucked." After he has put a speculum in her vagina while penetrating her anally, he says: "Hurts a little bit, doesn't it? I don't give a fuck, you little cunt."

While it's tempting to see Hardcore as a fringe character, his movies are for sale on most of the major pornography websites and he has a loyal fan base. On one of the websites dedicated to his work, which charges a $34.95 monthly fee for access, a fan writes, "We only dream of having sex like this, Max does it every day and with the passion of a true artist!"[27]

Certain companies make the industry nervous as well, such as Extreme Associates, which markets films that include rape scenarios, and JM Productions. JM owner Jeff Steward declares, proudly, "I don't follow trends. I create them."[28] One trend he's most proud of is what he calls "aggressive throat fucking" videos, such as his Gag Factor series, which has inspired a number of imitators. A typical description of a scene from the website:

> ONE OF THE BIGGEST WHORES EVER! Bridgette [Kerkove] will probably go down in the anals of porn history as one of the most filthy, disgusting cumpigs ever to have lived. She'll stuff as many cocks in her mouth, ass, and cunt as is physically possible—and then some! Check out this early Gag Factor scene, it's definitely a walk down memory lane![29]

When companies such as JM push into areas that seem taboo and are successful, the industry is quick to follow. Other gonzo producers pick up on the trend, and eventually the same acts can make their way in some form into features. The products of such a company can suggest the direction of the industry. This worries some in the industry who are concerned about the harshness of some of the gonzo pornography. LGI Digital CEO Bo Kenney told the industry's trade magazine that he doesn't want to shoot anything "overly rough":

> You do not have to degrade women for your product to sell. You need hot sex, and sex is all about fantasy. You need to make quality movies, not ultra-hardcore, degrading movies. Ultra-hardcore leaves the consumer empty, still longing for more degrading product, which gets producers in trouble with the government.[30]

So, there is hard-core (not degrading) and ultra-hardcore (degrading)—the good and the bad. Here are descriptions of two LGI Digital releases in 2005, which one assumes Kenney would describe as not degrading:

> "Cum Eating Teens"—These teens are craving man goo, and we all know the only way to get it! They will bend over backwards and suck that cock until they have sucked every last drop out of those big hard meat poles. Join the party as every girl takes a load in her mouth and swallows every last drop!

> "Pump that Rump"—All that empty space in her ass and nothing to put in it. Until he got a hold of her, now she'll be having cum drip out of her for a week. Camilla always said she liked her ass better when there was something in it.

INFINITE ARE THE WAYS WE CAN BE CRUEL

Hard-core pornography, whether ultra or otherwise, raises a question: Why do so many pornographic movies include scenes in which the women appear to be in pain?

To explore that question, it is not necessary to reach definitive conclusions about the degree of pain women actually experience in such scenes. My focus here is not on the women in the movie, but on the producers and consumers. In these scenes, the women appear to the viewer to be in pain. Their facial expressions and voices convey that the sex acts cause physical discomfort and/or fear and/or distress. Given the ease with which video can be edited, why did the producers not edit out those expressions? There are two possible answers. One, they may view these kinds of expressions of pain by the women as of no consequence to the viewers' interest, and hence of no consequence to the goal of maximizing sales; women's pain is neutral. The second possibility is that the producers have reason to believe that viewers like the expressions of pain; women's pain helps sales.

Given that the vast majority of those who will rent or buy these tapes are men, from that we can derive this question: Why do some men find the infliction of pain on women during sexual activity either (1) not an obstacle to their ability to achieve sexual pleasure or (2) a factor that can enhance their sexual pleasure? Phrased differently: Why are some men so callous and cruel sexually?

By that, I don't mean to ask why are men capable of being cruel in some general sense. All humans—men and women—have the capacity to be cruel toward other humans and other living things, and we all have done cruel things in our lives, myself included. Contemporary mainstream heterosexual pornography raises the question: Why do some men find cruelty to women either sexually neutral or sexually pleasurable?

Feminist research into, and women's reflection upon, experiences of sexual violence long ago established that rape involves the sexualization of power, the fusing in men's imaginations of sexual pleasure with domination and control. The common phrase "rape is about power, not sex" misleads; rape is about the fusion of sex and domination, about the eroticization of control. And in this culture, rape is normal. That is, in a culture where the dominant definition of sex is the taking of pleasure from women by men, rape is an expression of the sexual norms of the culture, not a violation of those norms. Sex is a sphere in which men are trained to see themselves as naturally dominant and women as naturally passive. Rape is both nominally illegal and completely normal at the same time, which is why men can engage in self-described behavior that meets the legal definition of rape and be certain they have never raped anyone.

So, it's not surprising that some pornography includes explicit images of women in pain. But a healthy society would want to deal with that, wouldn't it? Mainstream heterosexual pornography is getting more, not less, cruel. A healthy society would take such things seriously, wouldn't it? Let's take those questions seriously. Why is pornography so cruel?

There are only so many ways human beings can, in mechanical terms, have sex. There are a limited number of body parts and openings, a limited number of ways to create the friction that produces the stimulation and sensations, a limited number of positions from which the friction can be produced. Sexual variation, in this sense, is finite because of these physical limits.

Sex, of course, also has an emotional component, and emotions are infinitely variable. There are only so many ways people can rub bodies together, but endless are the ways different people can feel about rubbing bodies together in different times, places, and contexts. When most non-pornographic films, such as a typical Hollywood romance, deal with sex they draw on the emotions most commonly connected with sex—love and affection. But pornography doesn't, because films that exist to provide sexual stimulation for men in this culture wouldn't work if the sex were presented in the context of loving and affectionate relationships. Men typically consume pornography specifically to avoid love and affection. That means pornography has a problem. When all emotion is drained from sex it becomes repetitive and uninteresting, even to men who are watching primarily to facilitate masturbation. Because the novelty of seeing sex on the screen eventually wears off, pornography needs an edge. Pornography has to draw on some emotion, hence the cruelty.

When the legal restrictions on pornography slowly receded through the 1970s and 80s, and the presentation of sex on the screen was by itself no longer quite so illicit, pornography had to find that emotion. The more pornography becomes normalized and mainstreamed, the more pornography has to search for that edge. And that edge most commonly is cruelty, which emotionally is the easiest place to go for men, given that the dynamic of male domination and female submission is already in place in patriarchy.

FANTASY

When faced with this kind of critique, industry defenders typically retort with, "Pornography is just fantasy," implying there are no real-world effects of the material.

Yes, obviously, men fantasize when they use pornography. But just as obvious is that the scenes described in this chapter are not a fantasy. They are real. As Andrea Dworkin stressed over and over: Those acts that were filmed happened in the world; those things happened to those women; those women are not a fantasy.

And after those scenes were put on videotape, the films were sold and rented to thousands of men who took them home, put them into VCRs or DVD players, and masturbated to orgasm. That also is real. Men fantasize when they masturbate, but the men who are masturbating are not a fantasy. Thousands of men have climaxed to these images of women being aggressively throat fucked and penetrated by two men at the same time in ways that cause pain. Those orgasms happened in the real world, not in a fantasy world.

The argument that it's "just fantasy" implies that this particular form of mass media—unlike, say, news programs that affect our ideas about the world, or advertising that affects our buying habits—has no effects. That's an implausible claim on the surface, and one I'll explore in more depth later. But for now, for the sake of argument, let's assume pornography has no effects. One uncomfortable question remains:

If it's just fantasy, why these fantasies? Why fantasies of men's domination over women? Of women's subordination to men? Why fantasies of cruelty and degradation?

Even if it's just fantasies, what do these fantasies tell us not only about pornography, but about the world beyond pornography?

Can we look in that mirror?

choices, his and hers

[PRODUCTION]

A BRIEF OVERVIEW OF THE PORNOGRAPHY INDUSTRY

The first and most important thing to understand about the pornography industry is that it is an industry. The DVDs and internet sites to which men are masturbating are not being made by struggling artists who work in lonely garrets, tirelessly working to help us understand the mysteries of sexuality. In abstract discussions about sexually explicit material—the kind pornographers prefer we get lost in—a focus on the reality of pornography drifts off into musings about the nature of "sexual expression" that ponder the "transgressive" nature of pornography. Such discourse obscures the reality that the vast majority of pornography is produced to turn a profit, and those profits are substantial. The motive force of the industry is not exploration but exploitation.

Every modern communication technology ever devised—printing, photography, film, video, telephones, the internet, mobile communication devices—has become a vehicle for sexually explicit material. In the contemporary market, pornographers have found ways to make money off all those technologies. In a patriarchal society and capitalist economy, this shouldn't surprise us. Andrew Edmond—co-founder and former CEO of Flying Crocodile, a company that hosts adult entertainment websites and that at its peak employed 180 people[1]—put it bluntly:

> A lot of people [outside adult entertainment] get distracted from the business model by [the sex] and can't imagine anything complex about

| 79 |

it. Truth is, it's very complex. [Adult entertainment] is just as sophisticated and multilayered as any other marketplace. We operate just like any Fortune 500 company.[2]

While there are no absolutely reliable statistics on the industry's revenues, annual sales in the United States are commonly estimated at $10 billion or higher,[3] while worldwide revenues have been put at $57 billion.[4] For comparative purposes, the Hollywood box office—the amount of money Americans spent to go out to the movies—was $9 billion in 2005.[5] Because there is no way to chart the amount of money generated by pornographic websites, and other segments of the industry are almost as difficult to track, any estimates of the industry's revenues are rough and may well be low.

It is clear, however, that pornography in the post–World War II era has moved from a profitable underground business with ties to organized crime to become a profitable industry that operates openly and includes many small producers as well as corporations with substantial assets. Paul Thomas made that very point in crude fashion upon accepting the award for best director at the industry's 2005 awards ceremony by joking: "I used to get paid in cash by Italians. Now I get paid with a check by a Jew."

Increasingly, mainstream media corporations profit as well. Through ownership of cable distribution companies and internet services, the large companies that distribute pornography also distribute mainstream media. One example is News Corp., owned by Rupert Murdoch. Until it sold its stake in 2006 to Liberty Media (another mainstream media conglomerate), News Corp. was a major owner of DirecTV, which sells more pornographic films than *Hustler* publisher Larry Flynt.[6] Among News Corp.'s other media holdings are the Fox broadcasting and cable TV networks, 20th Century Fox, the *New York Post*, and *TV Guide*. Welcome to synergy: Murdoch also owns HarperCollins, which published pornography star Jenna Jameson's best-selling book.[7]

Recognizing the corporate-capitalist nature of the pornography industry is crucial to a second important point: The pornography we see today is distinct from the sexual images of other periods in human history. In an attempt to derail any criticism of the industry, pornographers and their supporters often argue that "there has always been pornography," from the time early humans drew on the walls of caves. While it's true that throughout human history there have been representations of sex in art and literature—from cave paintings to modern movies—it is not the case that all those representations have been the same or played the same role in society. To put that vast array of representations into one category leads people to think that all are equivalent, which is an absurd claim.

One obvious difference is in scale. In 2005, 13,588 new hard-core video/DVD titles were released, a number that has risen steadily since statistics were first kept.[8] Another difference is in the level of misogyny. While many types of images throughout human history have objectified, marginalized, or denigrated women,[9] there is nothing comparable to the deluge of woman-hating products of the contemporary pornography industry. Is there a cave painting that comes close to the conception of sex and gender in *Two in the Seat #3*?

As we move from cave paintings to the contemporary period, two specific technological developments deserve special attention—the home videocassette recorder and the internet. The availability of pornography on videotapes that could be played at home on a VCR was "probably the most revolutionary change in our business," according to Philip D. Harvey, founder and president of Adam & Eve and one of the most well-known pornographers.[10] Instead of having to go out to a theater, consumers could view pornography at home, part of the reason for the explosion of pornographic video production in the 1980s and 90s. The internet allows that same in-home privacy, only with instant delivery of a huge range of images. Anecdotal evidence suggests that the ease of clicking from one site and image to the next can lead to addictive-like behavior, something pornographers are aware of and seek to exploit to increase profits.[11]

The success of the pornography industry can be seen in its influence in technological choices. A number of commentators have argued that in the 1980s, Betamax lost out to VHS in the struggle over which videocassette recorder format would dominate, in part because the pornography industry went with VHS. In recent years, the pornography industry's choice of Blu-ray over HD-DVD may determine, or at least contribute to determining, the high-definition format for the next generation.[12] Though there are no doubt many commercial websites that have not made a profit, it's a virtual truism among technology watchers that pornography played a similarly crucial role in the development of the internet. As one online industry trade magazine put it in 2006:

> For years, the adult market has led online sales by providing the market with hundreds of thousands of choices and has rightfully led the way in selling content online. Subscription models, affiliate programs and many other new business modes were either invented or perfected by the adult webmaster. ... As recently as five years ago, the adult market produced 75 percent of all cash that was spent with online services.[13]

In the 2000s, the technology attracting ever-more attention has been mobile devices—cell phones, iPods, and other digital-video communication tools. If history is a guide, pornographers will find whatever ways there are to turn a profit by providing sexually explicit content and as a result there will be more pornography moving into more places than ever before. The logic of patriarchy and capitalism makes that expansion inevitable without intervention by feminist and/or left social movements.

Though there are many other technical and business aspects of the pornography industry to explore, I want to focus most of my attention on the most basic aspect of the production of pornography: the women who perform.

IT'S WHAT WOMEN ARE GOOD FOR

The most common strategy people use to try to bury the feminist anti-pornography critique is the trump card of "choice." Because the women in pornography choose to perform, many argue, there can be no critique of the industry. Here's how one male pornography user put it in an e-mail message to me:

> While reading your article there is one thing that I really wanted to point out to you. It's something I've always wanted to scream at all the feminists out there who hate pornography. *No one makes the girls do it.* They choose to do it.

And they get paid to do it. Some of them get paid quite well. In fact, the ones that don't get paid that well are still making a lot of money for the little amount of time it takes to make a porno. (Italics in the original)

This sums up the standard way in which men (and some women) derail any call for critical self-reflection about their use of pornography. After nearly two decades of public speaking and writing about this issue, I have heard the argument countless times after presentations. Men's standard formulation of the argument, as reflected in that comment, contains three assertions and one unstated assumption:

Assertion 1: The women in pornography choose it.

Assertion 2: They get paid a lot.

Assertion 3: Those who don't get paid a lot still have it easy because they are being paid for just getting fucked, which is easy, and besides …

Assumption: That's what women are for, to get fucked.

Before getting to an analysis of the concept of choice and the choices women make, I want to tell a story from the 2005 *Adult Video News* awards ceremony, the equivalent of the Academy Awards for the pornography industry, which is held each year at the AEE. That year I was at the convention as part of the crew of a documentary about the industry, and although we weren't allowed in to film the awards ceremony, I managed to find my way into the hotel ballroom for the convention's big finale. On my way out after the event, I happened to walk next to Cytherea, winner of the award for best new starlet. Cytherea is best known for squirting, or visible female ejaculation, a new trend in pornography in the past decade (though there is a debate as to whether the practice is real or simply women urinating during sex). This is how Cytherea's website describes her:

She likes her sex rough and she likes it dirty. … Aside from her squirting ability Cytherea is a Teen Dream. She is naturally beautiful with natural perky breasts. Cytherea has her pussy pierced and a butterfly tattoo, that adorn her sexy teen body. Her amazing ability for deep throating cock is also high up there on her resume of porn talents. She is very into getting fucked hard while she squirts all over her porn partner as well.[14]

As we walked along the rope line, with fans calling out to Cytherea, I fell in next to a woman who I guessed, correctly, was her mother. As she held her daughter's hand tightly, I asked her how she felt. She said she was very proud of her daughter. We walked a few more steps. Then, without really thinking, I asked her a question. In retrospect, it was a question I had no right to ask her, and I wish I could take it back. But at that point, late in the evening after a long day, without thinking much about it, I asked her, "When your daughter was a little girl, did you ever imagine this?" She turned to me with a look of horror on her face and said, "My god, no. Who would?"

I am a parent. I understood the reaction of Cytherea's mother. She was a mother—walking next to her daughter, whom she loved no doubt as much as any parent loves a child—listening to strange men shout things such as "Cytherea, I love you" and "Cytherea, show us your tits" and "Cytherea, I love to watch you squirt." Who could imagine such a fate for their daughter?

But Cytherea *chose* a career in pornography. And her mother *chose* to support her daughter. So, what does choice mean?

CHOICES, OBJECTIVE AND SUBJECTIVE

Like many concepts, we use "choice" in everyday conversation as if it were a simple matter. It isn't.

Let's start with an easy example: In my large lecture classes, I give multiple-choice exams. I do this not because I like them but because, with 150 to 300 students in a class, I need some data on which I can base a decision about assigning grades. Even with the help of teaching assistants, who grade a limited number of writing assignments, I cannot adequately assess that many students in a semester. So, I create numbers through these exams to provide the illusion of reasonable criteria for the grades I assign at the end of the term.

None of this, of course, fools the students; few of them believe that such exams are an accurate or meaningful way to measure their learning. Despite this understanding of the inadequacy of multiple-choice exams, all my students "choose" to take a test they know to be virtually useless. They choose to take that exam because if they were to choose not to—no matter how sensible and compelling their analysis of the exam's flaws—they would not pass the course, and they would be denied something that is important to them, a college diploma in a specific field they want to pursue (because the two large lecture courses I teach are required in my department, no student can receive a journalism degree without completing them).

Of course they could choose to reject the institution's demand, but that would mean giving up the benefits (whatever they may be, real or illusory) of a journalism degree from the University of Texas at Austin. Their choice is free, in the sense that no one is threatening them with direct harm if they choose differently, but it is not made under conditions of complete freedom, given their limited power in the system. So, does it make sense to say the students in my course "chose" to take a multiple-choice exam? Yes, of course it does, and yet it's more complicated than that.

But our analysis of choice can't stop there. We have to distinguish between the objective conditions in which people choose and their subjective understanding of those conditions.

For example, take a prisoner in a maximum-security correctional facility. When an order is given by a prison guard—a person who is heavily armed, reinforced by a large number of other heavily armed guards within striking distance, working in an institution that gives the guards and their superiors all formal power, in a society that is noticeably hostile to those incarcerated—it's not surprising that the vast majority of prisoners are going to choose to follow that order. Individual prisoners could choose to defy the order, but that choice would be made with the knowledge that they would suffer for it. Given those conditions, no one claims that prisoners have made a meaningful choice when they follow the guard's order, though of course any prisoner willing to endure the consequences could refuse to capitulate. In this case, the conditions are such that virtually everyone, in the same position, would follow that order. The vast majority of people wouldn't risk disobeying it, at least not without a sense that the entire prison population would support them, which would change the evaluation of risk.

Let's take another use of the idea of being a prisoner—when a woman feels like she's a prisoner in her own home, when a husband engages in controlling behavior. He monitors her every move, committing or threatening to commit violence if she goes anywhere without his permission. She was raised to believe that a wife should, whenever possible, follow the lead of the husband. She is economically dependent on him and, after many years of his constant denigration of her, has come to believe she could not support herself. And she is afraid—not without reason, given his outbursts of violence in the past—that if she doesn't do what he demands, he might hurt or even kill her. In this case, the conditions are such that some people would stay and some would leave; the way anyone balances the risk in leaving with the cost of staying will vary, depending on many factors, some internal to the individual and some in the larger world.

In the case of the prisoner and prison guard, no one would make the argument that the prisoner really chooses to follow the guard's orders, in the sense of a choice that is meaningfully free and uncoerced. The objective conditions of the prison are relatively uncomplicated, and the power residing in the prison administration is imposed without pretense. Virtually everyone's subjective assessment of the situation would be roughly the same.

In the case of the woman and an abusive partner, the term "prisoner" is not meant literally, in a legal sense, but as metaphor. It can be understood as metaphor, however, precisely because there is a sense in which we all can recognize that she is a prisoner of sorts. That is, no matter what our subjective assessment of her choices may be—we may see that she can get a court injunction, seek help from a battered women's shelter, or take other steps to expand her options—it's not difficult to see how her subjective assessment of her options would lead her to feel she has no real choice. She is, in that sense, every bit as much a prisoner as the person in jail. How she perceives her choices matters.

Reflection on our own lives quickly reveals that what might be called completely free choices are rare; every choice is made under some mix of real-world constraints and opportunities. From the prisoner examples, we can see the importance to a discussion of choice of how any particular individual perceives those constraints and opportunities.

EVALUATING CHOICES

So, let's return to the pornography consumer's invocation of women's choice as a defense to concerns about a critique of pornography.

A meaningful discussion of choice can't be restricted to the single moment when a woman decides to perform in a specific pornographic film but must include all the existing background conditions that affect not only the objective choices she faces but her subjective assessment of those choices. There is not much systematic research specifically on the women who perform in pornography. But from research and the testimony of women who have been prostituted—some of whom also are used in pornography—we know that childhood sexual assault (which often leads victims to see their value in the world primarily as the ability to provide sexual pleasure for men) and economic hardship (a lack of meaningful employment choices at a livable wage) are key factors in many women's decisions to enter the sex industry.[15] We know how women in the sex industry—not all, but many—routinely dissociate to cope with what they do; in one study of 130 street prostitutes, 68 percent met the diagnostic criteria for post-traumatic stress disorder.[16] We also know that pimps often use coercion and violence to keep women working as prostitutes. In the words of one team that reviewed research from nine countries, prostitution is "multitraumatic."[17]

Are women working under such conditions making a meaningful choice? There is no simple answer to that question. Recognizing the complexity does not mean we are treating the women like children, or ignoring their agency, or constructing them as dupes with no self-awareness. It is simply recognizing the reality of the world in which we live and they work, and at the very least it should give pause to those who want to make glib assertions about choice. Even if the women performing in pornography do not work under conditions as harsh as women prostituted on the street, the general outline of the argument remains the same. Where does that lead consumers as they evaluate how women's choices should affect their choices to use pornography?

For the sake of argument, let's assume that a specific woman in the sex industry has made a completely free and meaningful choice to participate, with absolutely no constraints or limitations on her, as women in the industry often assert. That could be the case, but it does not change the patterns described above, and the unavoidable conclusion that some number of women in the industry—likely a majority, and quite possibly a significant majority—choose under conditions that make choice complicated. And in most cases, the consumer has no reliable way to judge which women are participating in the industry as a result of a meaningfully free choice. When a consumer plays a DVD at home, he has no information that could help him make such a judgment. Therefore, he most likely is using a woman whose choice to perform was not meaningfully free.

But what if one did have information about the nature of the conditions, objective and subjective, under which the women made that choice?[18] Even then, the matter is not so simple. So long as the industry is profitable and a large number of women are needed to make such films, it is certain that some number of those women will be choosing under conditions that render the concept of "free choice" virtually meaningless. When a man buys or rents a DVD, he is creating the demand for pornography that will lead to some number of women being used—that is, being hurt in some fashion, psychologically and/or physically—no matter what he knows or thinks he knows about a specific woman.

So, men's choices to buy or rent pornography are complicated by two facts. First, he can't know the conditions under which women made their choices, and hence can't know how meaningful the choices were. And second, even if he could make such a determination about specific women in a specific film he watches, the demand for pornography that his purchase helps create ensures that some women will be hurt.

Logically, that argument is clear. But whether one accepts these arguments depends in part on one's capacity for empathy. Because we live in a world in which it is so easy to detach, to isolate ourselves from others, we have to work at empathy, that most fundamental of human qualities. We have to remind ourselves to exercise our ability to connect our humanity with another, to travel to that person's world and to try to feel along with another human being.

There is a genre of gonzo films that focus on women performing oral sex on men, some of which feature rough treatment of the women. One variety is called a "blow bang," in which a woman has oral sex in similar fashion with more than one man. In one of these films, *Blow Bang #4*, released in 2001, a young woman dressed as a cheerleader is surrounded by six men. At the outset of her scene, "Dynamite" (the name she gives on tape) says, "I'm a little shy." The off-camera interviewer replies, "Don't be shy. I've got some candy for you. Good whore. You're going to six guys today. Aren't you a brave little cheerleader?" After about seven minutes, Dynamite methodically moves man to man, performing oral sex on them while they offer such as "you little cheerleading slut." Other comments the men in this scene include:

> That's it you little bitch, suck that cock. Share your pretty fucking mouth. Welcome to Blow Bang you whore. Yes, gag you little bitch, to the balls. Yeah, spit up, you little baby. Yes, the cocks love you. You like all the attention, don't you little girl. Filthy fucking cock slut. You are going to cheer for us, you little bitch. You're going to take six for the team. Choke on it. Yes, aren't you popular. Now we know why you're the popular cheerleader. You're not done yet, little girl. You're not done until you give a gift, until you puke. [*She gags.*] Now you're speaking our language.

For another minute and a half, Dynamite sits upside down on a couch, her head hanging over the edge, while men thrust into her mouth, causing her to gag. She strikes the pose of the bad girl to the end. "You like coming on my pretty little face, don't you," she says, as they ejaculate on her face and in her mouth for the final two minutes of the scene.

Five men have finished. The sixth steps up. As she waits for him to ejaculate onto her face, now covered with semen, she closes her eyes tightly and grimaces. For a moment, her face changes; it is difficult to read her emotions, but it appears she may cry. After the last man, number six, ejaculates, she regains her composure and smiles. Then the narrator off camera hands her the pom-pom she had been holding at the beginning of the tape and says, "Here's your little cum mop, sweetheart—mop up." She buries her face in the pom-pom and the scene ends.

The women in the movement to end men's violence have helped society understand that we have to empathize with the victims of sexual assault and domestic violence. We need to extend that empathy to the women in pornography and prostitution. Here's the first thing to remember in that process: Dynamite is one of us. She is a person. She has hopes and dreams and desires of her own.

Let's linger on a specific moment in that scene with Dynamite. After she has performed oral sex on six men, after six men have thrust their penises into her throat to the point of gagging her, after six men have ejaculated onto her, the camera is turned off. Close your eyes and think not about the sex acts but about the moment after the sex, when the camera shuts off. The men walk away. Someone throws her a towel. She has to clean the semen of six strangers off her face and body and from her hair. This woman—who is a person, who is one of us, who has hopes and dreams and desires of her own—cleans herself off.

Imagine that the woman in that scene is your child. How would you feel if the woman being handed a towel to wipe off the semen of six men were your child, someone you had raised and loved and cared for? Imagine that woman is the child of your best friend, or of your neighbor, or of someone you work with. Then imagine that woman is the child of someone you have never met and never will meet. Imagine that woman is just a person, one of us, with hopes and dreams and desires of her own. Forget about whether or not she is your child. Just remember that she is a person; she is one of us.

Now, imagine that you are the one handing her the towel. Could you dare to look into her eyes? We need to dare to look into her eyes and try to understand what she might be feeling. We can't know for sure what she is feeling, but we can try to imagine how we might feel if we were in her position.

Even pornography producers have the capacity to understand these questions, though they turn away from them. John Stagliano, founder of Evil Angel and originator of the popular Buttman series, acknowledged that in a 2002 interview, discussing some of the directors who are shooting rougher sex:

The biggest problem with the porn business is that as a producer, I still feel responsible if a girl gets her ass hurt by Christoph Clark [a director whose films Evil Angel distributes] in Eastern Europe or if Joey [Silvera, another director whose films are distributed by Evil Angel] pushes a girl a little bit too far and she thinks it was an unpleasant experience. Most of the time those things don't happen or I wouldn't be doing business with those people. Most of the time it's a positive experience for these girls. The problem is that we are paying them to do harder sex, we are rewarded financially to do weirder and weirder stuff. There is a financial incentive to ask these girls to try it. Sometimes they try it and they don't like it. That's unfortunate and that's my biggest problem with the porno business today. Having a family, I am more aware of it now, but I try and keep my perspective and understand that it's just porn. Everyone is here voluntarily and everyone is just playing around. There are risks involved and we will deal with those risks.[19]

At some level, Stagliano seems to understand the question, but he turns away. But what if we practiced that empathy? Then what might we say about Dynamite? Would our first reaction be, "Well, she chose to be there"? Or would we want to talk to her, away from the pornographers, in some setting where we could talk like human beings, where we could understand her more deeply, as a person with hopes and dreams? I can't know what Dynamite might tell us, of course. To empathize, I don't have to pretend to know more, or know better, than Dynamite knows about her own life. We can listen to what she says—her words, not the pornographers' script, spoken in a setting where she is truly free to speak. We can put those comments into a broader context of what we know about women in the sex industry. And as we do that, we can try to put ourselves in her place, surrounded by those six men. We can ask ourselves if we would want to be there, or if we would want our loved ones to be there. And, if our answer is we would rather not, we can ponder why that is.

None of that would undermine the agency of Dynamite or treat her like a dupe. It would simply deepen our ability to feel and understand and reason our way through a complex world. When we engage with another empathically, we recognize a connection. We know we are not disrespecting the other person because it doesn't feel like that; it feels caring, not judgmental. We also can recognize when we aren't in empathetic connection with another. Sometimes we can see in others that same failure to empathize.

WHAT NON-EMPATHY LOOKS LIKE

The DVD features of *Big Booty White Girls*, a 2004 gonzo release from Evil Angel, include a commentary track, on which viewers can hear the voices of director/performer Justin Slayer and the cameraman, commenting on the scene over the regular soundtrack. In the scene with Melanie Crush, the combination of the images and commentary is the crystallization of the death of empathy.

Although it isn't clear where Crush is from or what her native language is, it appears that she speaks very little English, and she says nothing beyond a few words. The sex begins with Slayer performing oral sex on her, and she makes sounds of pleasure. She then gets on her knees, facing the back of the couch, and he enters her vaginally from the rear, holding on to her hair while he thrusts. At this point, her vocalizations start to become unclear; it's difficult to tell if they are moans of pleasure or pain. When he thrusts all the way in, her vocalizations and facial expressions begin to sound and look more clearly pained. As this continues, he says, "You like getting fucked like that? You want some more?" She doesn't answer. He then penetrates her anally, in varying positions. He asks her if it's good, and for the first time she says yes. As he thrusts into her anus, she touches her vagina. As he thrusts faster, the pace at which she touches herself drops off and, again, she seems to be in pain. He then tells her he is going to go deep. She seems clearly to be in pain, her eyes closed, as she reaches back for something to grab hold of. He says, "Look at me. I'm fucking your ass. Look at me. Look at me." He kisses her and begins thrusting again, at which point her expression leaves no doubt that he is hurting her. Her hands reach out to brace herself against him. Without a lot of warning, he ejaculates on her face and in her mouth. At this point, with his penis out of her, she seems to come back to life.

We all recognize that there are certain vocalizations and expressions that people display during sexual activity that are ambiguous; they could be read as markers of pleasure or pain. But in this scene, there were many moments in which it is difficult to interpret Crush's responses as anything other than expressions of pain. Perhaps no one other than Crush can know that, but my point is simply that to an observer, she seems to clearly be in pain many times during this scene.

In the commentary track, we see how the men making the film interpreted those vocalizations and facial expressions:

> Cameraman: What I like about her, too, Dog, was performance stopped for her when you touched her. She was for real, wanting to fuck. She was playing out her personal fantasy. ... Her eyes, to me, man. You see the expression on her face, like, you know what, "I'm really, I'm really enjoying this." You know what, it almost made me feel like she really needed to fuck. Like she needed to get fucked. Because you know a lot of those pretty chicks, a lot of them pretty chicks are not getting fucked.

> Justin Slayer: You got to be in tune with the chick. That's the universal language right there. ... That little squealing like a little pig she's doing. ...

> C: I've learned that if you can get the chick into it, she'll do just about any damn thing. Because she's got to relax and shit. ... Because they're made to get fucked like that. I mean, why else would her ass be that fat, her pussy look like that, her thighs look like that? She looked like that because she was made to get fucked. ... Who can say they ain't made for that.

> JS: She did squat on down [during anal penetration]. She likes it. [*She screams, clearly in pain.*] Oh, went a little too deep.

C: Now you see what's really real. We cut all the Hollywood shit out. You saw what's really real.

Just as there is no way to know for sure what Melanie Crush was experiencing, there's no way to know how much of the commentary between Slayer and the cameraman reflected what they believe and feel about the scene. But their comments are either an honest account of their own perceptions or an account constructed for the viewers. Either they believe, or they want the men watching to believe, that (1) women are physically and emotionally designed to be used sexually in this fashion; (2) they enjoy it; and (3) expressions that appear to indicate the woman is in discomfort and pain either are not recognized or interpreted as expressions of pleasure.

What does Justin Slayer really think, and how does that influence the movies he makes? I wouldn't begin to claim to know. But here's how he described his work to an interviewer in 2005:

> Justin Slayer: Right now I am working on *Mami Culo Grande*. "Mami" is a little Latin girl. We call them "Mami's." And the "culo" is the ass. "Grande" means big. So now we have the big booty Latin girls line. I also have my *Black Pipe Layer* movie coming out. That's one of my signature series where we just completely wreck little white girls—DP, Anal and just stretch them all open.
>
> Steve C.: For those who don't already know, could you explain what DP is?
>
> JS: DP is double penetration. You fuck a girl in her ass and her pussy at the same time. You know what I mean? That's what we do.
>
> SC: That sounds awfully painful.
>
> JS: I don't know about pain and shit. I have never experienced that.
>
> SC: What I mean is that there is a girl underneath screaming her head off.
>
> JS: Yeah sometimes. But there's also some girls that can take that shit. There's some girls that

want nothing under that, you know what I mean? We're dealing with professionals here, this is porno. This is the mother fuckin' NBA, NFL of mother fuckin' freaks. There's some freaky shit goin' on.[20]

There is, indeed, some freaky shit going on, in the world of pornography and beyond.

This chapter has focused on the people performing, and understanding the conditions under which they perform is a crucial aspect of a political and ethical evaluation of the pornography industry. As Andrea Dworkin put it, "pornography happens to women."[21] By that, she meant that what consumers watch on a screen happened in the world to a real woman. She also meant that in the world, pornography gets used by men, which has effects on the lives of real women in the world. So, a complete assessment requires that we move from the question of production to consumption.

we are what we masturbate to

[CONSUMPTION]

The first and most important thing to understand about men's use of pornography is that it involves men using pornography. By that, I mean that the consumers of contemporary mass-marketed heterosexual pornography are overwhelmingly male, and that they do not simply view pornography but use it, as a masturbation facilitator. Those two realities are crucial to any inquiry into the effects of pornography on attitudes and behaviors.

The pornography industry acknowledges the role of its products in men's masturbation. For example, an *Adult Video News* story on gonzo directors sums up the reasons for the genre's popularity with producers and consumers:

> Gonzo, non-feature fare is the overwhelmingly dominant porn genre since it's less expensive to produce than plot-oriented features, but just as importantly, is the fare of choice for the solo stroking consumer who merely wants to cut to the chase, get off on the good stuff, then, if they really wanna catch some acting, plot and dialog, pop in the latest Netflix disc. These shooters [directors] understand that, and for that, we salute them.[1]

The industry is well aware that the typical "solo stroking consumer" is a man, but it likes to tell the story that women are just as interested in pornography as men—or, at least, would be if they could shake off the repressive attitudes of a puritanical society. Some in the industry argue women would then embrace the same kind of pornography men like; others suggest a more "women-centered" pornography is necessary.

As with many other questions about pornography, there is no reliable data on the male-female breakdown for pornography use. But whatever one believes women should think and feel about sexuality and pornography, it is clear that contemporary pornography predominantly reflects the male sexual imagination rooted in a dominant conception of masculinity: sex as control, conquest, domination, and the acquisition of pleasure by the taking of women. In my interviews over the past decade with pornography producers and sellers, I have always asked what percentage of their customers are men. The lowest figure anyone has ever given me is 80 percent, though all acknowledge that more women view pornography today than even a decade ago as sexually explicit material becomes more normalized. So, my focus in this chapter will be on pornography's relationship to men's attitudes about women and sex, and men's behavior with women in sexual and nonsexual situations.

A skeptical reader might ask: How can you be sure there is a relationship between pornography use and attitudes and/or behavior? One can't be sure, of course, without evidence and a theory to make sense of the evidence. But many people assume there is a connection, including the "father of gonzo," John "Buttman" Stagliano.

PORNOGRAPHY AND "A PSYCHOLOGY THAT I DON'T THINK IS HEALTHY"

At the 2006 Adult Entertainment Expo, I asked Stagliano if the gonzo pornography that portrayed ever rougher and more extreme sex worried him for any reason. He said that while he would never say the industry is heading in the wrong direction, "there's a lot more harder-edged stuff; there's a lot more stuff that I would consider unpleasant to look at, that I personally don't like." He quickly emphasized that the movies commonly criticized—such as Extreme Associate's films with rape scenarios[2]—were made with the full consent of all involved and, therefore, should be legal without question. But on the deeper question of what such films reflect about the culture and how they might affect people, he equivocated, saying, "I find that maybe feeds into a psychology that I don't think is healthy. But

I don't really know that it's unhealthy. And for some people it may be a healthy thing."

What is the "psychology" that he isn't so sure about? Stagliano explained:

> The psychology is that some people like to abuse other people, in real life, in real situations. And I worry that we're creating art that feeds on that, that kind of reinforces that and says it's a good thing, and makes people a little more comfortable with certain psychological things that I think they should be uncomfortable with because they're bad.

So, the father of gonzo (which is "art," in his view) is concerned that the more extreme varieties of pornography could possibly reinforce and normalize attitudes that legitimate abuse. And if one is concerned about the effects of the roughest and harshest forms of pornography, well, then logically one should be concerned about the effects of all the industry's products, since there's no reason to assume that only the most extreme pornography might have such an effect.

In other words, in a candid moment, the head of one of the most well-known pornography production and distribution companies acknowledged what feminist critics have said for decades: A connection between men's use of misogynistic pornography and sexual violence is plausible. No doubt, Stagliano would disagree with feminists about how clearly such a link has been established and what society should do if and when such links are definitively established. But it's crucial to recognize that his comments acknowledge the fact that such a link makes intuitive sense, something that the pornography industry has long denied in its "pornography is just fantasy" line.

There's an implicit assumption in Stagliano's position that the films he creates and/or distributes are significantly different from the "harder-edged stuff" that makes him nervous. But such a distinction is hard to justify when one looks closer.

Here's my summary of one scene featuring Krysti Lynn (once Stagliano's girlfriend) and Rocco Siffredi (one of the most well-known male stars in pornography) from the 1995 release *Buttman's Big Butt Backdoor Babes*, one of the films in the sample from my first study of video pornography:

Krysti "takes a meeting" with Rocco at the director's backyard pool. After running through the standard sequence of positions, Rocco tries to penetrate her anally but his first attempts fail, apparently due in part to the size of his penis, and as he pushes harder the camera shows her face with what seems clearly to be an expression of pain. Her "fuck me" talk gives way to a guttural sound of pain that sounds authentic. After a few minutes of anal sex, Rocco resumes vaginal intercourse before ejaculating onto her buttocks, slapping her buttocks with his penis, and spanking her. In the background, an ambulance siren on the street happened to be passing by, and the off-camera voice says, "Well, the ambulance is coming for you, Ms. Krysti Lynn. I know that was pretty rough." She then displays her anus and vagina for the camera, and the off-camera voice says, "Yeah, you've been worked over kid, pretty good."

Compare my description with the summary from a popular website for reviews of pornographic films, adultdvdtalk. com:

Krysti gives Rocco a blowjob and eats his ass (nasty)! She, then, shows her ass to Rocco & the rest of us (by camera). Rocco eats her pussy & ass while she moans and we hear sounds of helicopter whirring. He lubes up her ass with his saliva and fingers her. Rocco fucks her from behind and then he takes her reverse cowgirl & cowgirl. Later, Rocco fucks Krysti in the butt while she sticks a dildo in her pussy. Position Swap: Missionary. Krysti moans wildly and then she turns over again. Here's the usual: The cumshot. Rocco cums all over her ass and spanks her in between her ass with his dick. Good scene.[3]

In that scene, not only did no one stop the action when it appeared that Krysti Lynn was in pain, but the director displayed the physical evidence of that pain and joked about it.

Stagliano can see the potential for negative consequences in the most extreme contemporary pornography, but presumably doesn't see that same logic as applicable to his own directorial efforts or the work he distributes, which now includes Siffredi's work as a director and performer. (Siffredi is an unusual man in the pornography industry; in addition to this hard-core work, he has starred in a mainstream movie, *Anatomy of Hell*, directed by Catherine Breillat.) Here's how a pro-pornography reviewer for the *Village Voice* describe the "all-anal slutfest" film *Rocco: Animal Trainer 10*, released in 2002 by Stagliano's Evil Angel:

> In the first scene, centered on a seven-sided bed, Rocco videos an English-accented, anonymous buddy; Bella ("Ciao Bella!" the charming Rocco greets her), who wears a rather large buttplug under her micro denim shorts; the elegant, quiet Sara; and a blond dressed as a dominatrix, who gapes at Bella's gaping asshole and Buddy's uninvited slapping, choking, and face-fucking. Bella, who I've previously seen perform some of the filthier acts I've witnessed, takes the brunt of this abuse, with tears streaming down her cheeks—perhaps the simple physical result of having a large dick forcibly held down her throat—and an insistent, not entirely convincing smile on her face.[4]

Whatever Stagliano really thinks is healthy or not, he knows what sells. He knows that Rocco sells:

> I was the first to shoot Rocco. Together we evolved toward rougher stuff. He started to spit on girls. A strong male-dominant thing, with women being pushed to their limit. It looks like violence but it's not. I mean, pleasure and pain are the same thing, right? Rocco is driven by the market. What makes it in today's market place is reality.[5]

THE REALITY OF MAKING RAPE INVITING

Pornography's supporters evade the question of the effects of this material on attitudes and behavior by framing the question in simplistic terms: "Does pornography cause rape?" That one is easy to answer: No.

Since some men who use pornography don't rape, and some men who rape don't use pornography, pornography is neither a necessary nor sufficient condition for rape. There is no way to make a convincing claim that pornography is, as the lawyers say, an "if not but for" cause—"if not but for the use of pornography, this man would not have raped." This observation is easy; simplistic cause-and-effect models are never particularly useful in explaining human behavior. For example, what *causes* a student to cheat on a multiple-choice test? Fear of failing the exam? A dislike of the professor? An inherent character flaw? The motivations behind any human behavior are complex; talking about causes in simple terms is simplistic.

Let's move to a more useful question: "Is pornography ever a factor that contributes to rape?" That question recognizes the limits of humans' ability to understand complex behavior while at the same time opening up pathways for deeper understanding within those limits. Feminist critics of pornography do not argue that pornography is ever the sole direct causal agent in sexual violence. No one argues that if pornography were eliminated rape would disappear. Instead, the discussion should be about the ways in which pornography might be implicated in sexual violence in this culture. Pornography alone doesn't make men do it, but pornography is part of a world in which men do it, and therefore the production, content, and use of pornography are important to understand in the quest to eliminate sexual violence.

Most reviews of the research on the potential connections between pornography and sexual violence suggest that there is evidence of some limited effects on male consumers but no way to reach definitive conclusions. It's unlikely scientific research will ever be able to demonstrate a simple, direct causal link between the consumption of pornography and sexual violence. Human behavior involves too much complexity for it to be otherwise. If one is looking for direct causal links in a traditional science model, this is likely to be a permanent assessment; it is difficult to imagine research methods that could provide more compelling data and conclusions.

There's no way to isolate with any certainty the effect of one particular manifestation of misogyny (pornography) in a culture that is generally misogynistic. In fact, the danger of pornography is heightened exactly because it is only one part of a sexist system and because the message it carries about sexuality is reinforced elsewhere. What we learn from the testimony of women and men whose lives have been touched by pornography is how the material is implicated in violence against women and how it can perpetuate, reinforce, and be part of a wider system of woman-hating. Rather than discussing simple causation, we should consider how various factors, in feminist philosopher Marilyn Frye's terms, "make something inviting." In those terms, pornography does not cause rape but rather helps make rape inviting.

Three basic types of studies have been undertaken on the relationship between pornography and violence, two of which are within the traditional scientific model, and of limited value. First, a few large-scale studies have investigated the correlation of the availability of pornography to rates of violence, with mixed results.[6] The complexity of confounding variables and the imprecision of measures make these studies virtually useless.

Second, experimental studies in the laboratory have been constructed to investigate directly the question of causal links. A typical study might expose groups of subjects to different types or levels of sexually explicit material for comparison with a control group that views nonsexual material. Researchers look for significant differences between the groups on a measure of, for example, male attitudes toward rape. From such controlled testing—measuring the effect of an experimental stimulus (exposure to pornography) on a dependent variable (attitudes toward women or sex) in randomly selected groups—researchers make claims, usually tentative, about causal relationships.

One of the most thorough reviews of the experimental literature by leading researchers in the field concluded that "if a person has relatively aggressive sexual inclinations resulting from various personal and/or cultural factors, some pornography exposure may activate and reinforce associated coercive tendencies and behaviors."[7] The authors also pointed out that "high pornography use is not necessarily indicative of high risk for sexual aggression."[8] Another large-scale literature review also concluded that men predisposed toward violence are most likely to show effects and that men not predisposed are unlikely to show effects.[9]

While this experimental work sometimes offers interesting hints at how pornography works in regard to men's sexual behavior, it suffers from several serious problems that limit its value. First, the measures of men's attitudes toward women, such as answers to questions about the appropriate punishment for rapists, do not necessarily tell us anything about men's willingness to rape. Given that men often do not view their sexually aggressive or violent behavior as aggression or violence—to them, it's just sex—men who rape often condemn rape, which they see as something other men do. Also, sexual behavior is a complicated mix of cognitive, emotional, and physical responses, and the answers one gives to a survey may or may not accurately reflect that mix.

Most important, these lab studies are incapable of measuring subtle effects that develop over time. If pornography develops attitudes and shapes behavior after repeated exposure, there is no guarantee that studies exposing people to a small amount of pornography over a short time can accurately measure anything. For example, in one study, the group exposed to what the researchers called the "massive" category of pornography viewed six explicitly sexual, eight-minute films per session for six sessions, or a total of four hours and 48 minutes of material.[10] And, of course, no lab experiment can replicate the practice of masturbating to pornography, which no doubt influences the way in which men interpret and are affected by pornography. Orgasm is a powerful physical and emotional experience that is central to the pornographic experience, yet there is no ethical way that lab studies can take this into account. Although most pro-pornography critics of the experimental research caution that such studies may overstate the effects, for these reasons it is just as likely that the research underestimates pornography's role in promoting misogynistic attitudes and behavior.

A third method of investigation—interviews with men who use pornography, especially those who are sexually aggressive, and women involved in relationships with such men—can't promise conclusive scientific judgments about the effects of pornography, but such work can help us achieve a deeper understanding. It is especially important to include the experiences of women, the main targets of violence, who have crucial insights.

Based both on the lab research and such interviews, Diana Russell has argued that pornography is a causal factor in the way that it can:

» predispose some males to desire rape or intensify this desire;

» undermine some males' internal inhibitions against acting out rape desires;

» undermine some males' social inhibitions against acting out rape desires; and

» undermine some potential victims' abilities to avoid or resist rape.[11]

The public testimony of women,[12] my interviews with pornography users and sex offenders, and various other researchers' work, have led me to conclude that pornography can:

» be an important factor in shaping a male-dominant view of sexuality;

» be used to initiate victims and break down their resistance to sexual activity;

» contribute to a user's difficulty in separating sexual fantasy and reality; and

» provide a training manual for abusers.[13]

Consider the following reports and what they tell us about the relationship between pornography and behavior:

From a street prostitute, who reported that when one john exploded at her he said:

> I know all about you bitches, you're no different; you're like all of them. I seen it in all the movies. You love being beaten. [He then began punching the victim violently.] I just seen it again in that flick. He beat the shit out of her while he raped her and she told him she loved it; you know you love it; tell me you love it.[14]

Consider the reports from three different men in my study who had been convicted of sex offenses[15]:

From a 34-year-old man who had raped women and sexually abused girls:

There was a lot of oral sex that I wanted her to perform on me. There were, like, ways that would entice it in the movies, and I tried to use that on her, and it wouldn't work. Sometimes I'd get frustrated, and that's when I started hitting her. ... I used a lot of force, a lot of direct demands, that in the movies women would just cooperate. And I would demand stuff from her. And if she didn't, I'd start slapping her around.[16]

From a 41-year-old man who had sexually abused his stepdaughter:

In fact, when I'd be abusing my daughter, I'd be thinking about some women I saw in a video. Because if I was to open my eyes and see my stepdaughter laying there while I was abusing her, you know, that wouldn't have been very exciting for me. You know, that would bring me back to the painful reality that I'm a child molester, where I'm in this reality of I'm making love or having intercourse with this beautiful woman from the video. The video didn't even come into my mind. It was just this beautiful person who had a beautiful body, and she was willing to do anything I asked.[17]

From a 24-year-old man who had sexually abused young girls while working as a school bus driver:

When I was masturbating to these pornography things, I would think about certain girls I had seen on the bus or ones I had sold drugs to, and I would think as I was looking at these pictures in these books, what would it be like to have this girl or whoever doing this, what I'm thinking about. ... Just masturbating to the thought wasn't getting it for me anymore. I actually had to be a part of it, or actually had to do something about it. ... Like sometimes after I'd see like a certain load of kids would get off the bus, I'd pick out a couple and I'd watch them or stop and look at the mirror and stare at them and stuff like that. I would think, later on in the day, I'd masturbate to some pornography, I'd just use that picture kind of as a mental, it's kind of a scenery or whatever, and I'd put in my mind I'd put myself and whoever at the time I was thinking about, in that picture.[18]

"ORDINARY" RELATIONSHIPS AND "NORMAL" MEN

These stories focus on the relationship between pornography and sexual violence, the kind of sex that most everyone in the culture condemns. But an investigation into pornography's role in the world can't stop with only those actors and actions that are criminal. If we understand how the habitual use of pornography with misogynistic themes can be a factor in shaping the attitudes and behaviors of men who rape, we have to face an unavoidable question: What effect does it have on men who don't rape? That is, could the sexual attitudes of non-rapists also be affected? Could habitual use of pornography be a factor in shaping the attitudes of men that lead them to treat their consensual partners with callousness and disrespect? In a society in which men are already being taught in many other venues that sex is about conquest, control, and domination—could pornography that has those same values help reinforce such behaviors?

This has been a focus of the feminist critique of pornography from the start. In one of the first edited volumes that articulated the critique, a woman who had been interviewed in a study of sexual assault reported:

> My husband enjoys pornographic movies. He tries to get me to do things he finds exciting in movies. They include twosomes and threesomes. I always refuse. Also, I was always upset with his ideas about putting objects in my vagina, until I learned this is not as deviant as I used to think. He used to force me or put whatever he enjoyed into me.[19]

The same studies and stories that are cited in discussion of the connection between pornography and rape are just as relevant to questions about the effect of such material on the "ordinary" behavior of "normal" men. Those four effects described above—shaping a male-dominant view of sexuality, initiating victims, contributing to difficulty in separating sexual fantasy and reality, and providing a training manual for abusers—are at work just as much with men who have not engaged in activities that meet the legal definition of rape. Here we have to let go of a comforting illusion—that there is some clear line between men who rape and men who don't rape, between the bad guys and the good guys.

Rape is defined legally as penetration without consent.[20] In reading the section on rape in the Texas Penal Code, I am reasonably sure I have never violated that law. But I also realize that much of my sexual training as a man was about gaining women's consent to sex in whatever way one could. It's illegal to compel a woman "to submit or participate by the use of physical force or violence" to sex, but as a young man I was taught that sometimes you have to push a little harder when she at first says no, because she really wants it. It's illegal to impair a woman's judgment "by administering any substance without the other person's knowledge," but as a young man I was taught that sometimes you have to spike a woman's drink with extra liquor or encourage her to drink one more beer, just to get her in the mood. Like many young men, I was taught that a woman's "no" to sex could mean "no," or it could mean "maybe," or it could mean "yes, but you have to come get me." The only way to know if "no means no" was to push. Men push, and women either push back or give in. Even if I never played it particularly well, that's the game I was taught to play.

When I speak publicly in mixed groups, I sometimes make a joke about the routinely boorish sexual behavior of men—the tendency to focus on sex and ignore other aspects of intimacy, the relentless requests/demands for sex, the ways in which men try to corner women so that it is easier for women to engage in sex than keep resisting. I describe that and then say, "Of course I'm sure no women here today have ever experienced that." Immediately the women in the room either smile or laugh out loud. Often, the next thing many of them do is look around at the men in the room to see how they are reacting, to check on whether the men are angry. The women know what I'm talking about, and they also know it can be dangerous to acknowledge that in front of men, who typically don't like having those patterns pointed out.

When I speak in public, I always use the pronoun "we" when speaking about men. No matter what my feminist politics these days, I was raised to be a man, and that training doesn't magically disappear by reading feminist books. I have to examine my own past and evaluate how I behave today. This is a reminder that this analysis is not focused on some subset of the male population that can be identified and isolated from "normal" men. When people ask me what kind of men enjoy—which means, of course, enjoy masturbating to—pornography that is so clearly rooted in woman-hating, my answer is simple: Men like me. Men like all of us. Not all men, but men like all of us. Men who can't get a date as well as men who have all the dates they could want. Men who live alone and men who are married. Men who grew up in liberal homes in which pornography was never a big deal and men who grew up in strict religious homes in which no talk of sex was allowed. Black and white and brown and any-other-color-you-can-imagine men. Rich men and poor men.

For men, there can be no retreat to the category of "one of the good guys." Like most men, I like to think of myself as a good guy, and I suppose that compared with Howard Stern, I am. But somehow that's not terribly reassuring. I recognize that it's not as simple as lining up the good guys and bad guys and making sure you are on the right side of the line.

I am reasonably sure I have never violated the laws on sexual assault, that no partner of mine ever felt that I had engaged in sex without consent. But I am less sure that in my sexual life I have always avoided more subtle rape-like behavior, especially when I was younger and had yet to critically reflect on these rules for men's behavior that I was being taught. Was I ever sexual with a partner who didn't want to be sexual in that moment but consented simply because it was easier than whatever consequences she perceived would result from saying no? I cannot answer that with certainty, but I can guess. And as much as I wish I could say that never happened, I am reasonably sure that it did sometimes.

Even when there is explicit consent between a man and woman, there are questions we men should always ask ourselves. The most basic is the most troubling: In intimate moments with a partner during sex, are we engaged in a way that treats our partner like a human being, someone with hopes and dreams and desires of her own? Or are we engaged in a way that treats her like an object, like something—not someone—whose role in the world at that moment is to produce sexual pleasure for us?

Radical feminists are often alleged to believe that all sex between a man and a woman is rape, a caricature that is popular because it keeps us from that troubling question. Radical feminists refuse to accept the bad guys/good guys distinction. They don't claim every man is a rapist, but they do recognize that men in this society are raised in a rape culture and are shaped by that culture. Is that really so radical? Or is it simply honest?

If we decide to be honest, in radical fashion, another troubling question arises: When a man who thinks of himself as one of the good guys engages in the habitual use of misogynistic pornography, does it affect his attitude toward women and/or his sexual behavior?

Following the conclusions described earlier in this chapter, we might ask:

» Is it possible that a "good guy's" use of pornography could be a factor in shaping his imagination in ways that sexualize male dominance?

» Does a "good guy" ever try to get a female partner to watch pornography with him to undermine her resistance to particular sexual acts that he wants but that she rejects?

» Can regular use of pornography by a "good guy" make the line in his head between sexual fantasy and reality a bit blurry?

» Does habitual use of pornography, especially those movies that feature extreme sex acts, ever give a "good guy" ideas about, and desires for, specific sexual acts that are denigrating to women that he otherwise might not have ever considered?

And it's important to pose another question about "normal" men's use of pornography, especially in the internet age: Can the habitual use of pornography, given its addictive-like qualities, lessen men's ability to make meaningful intimate connections with a partner? That is, can pornography contribute not only to some men's aggressive sexual behavior, but also to other men's shutting down emotionally and physically, leaving partners feeling rejected?

Psychologist Ana Bridges, who specializes in the impact of pornography on romantic relationships,[21] has found that the research provides convincing evidence that pornography harms heterosexual relationships both indirectly, by affecting attitudes and emotions of viewers, and directly, by negatively influencing ratings and appraisals of a romantic partner. Bridges concludes:

> Studies on compulsive pornography use suggest that viewers habituate (become used to) certain images and sex acts, and thus require more and more deviant materials to achieve sexual arousal. My own research suggests that the harm created in relationships when one person uses pornography while the other does not can be substantial and devastating. Specifically, some women in relationships with male users of pornography reported feeling like their partners were fantasizing about a pornographic image or scene during intercourse rather than sharing that intimate moment with her. Other women stated that their partners were no longer seeking them out for lovemaking; instead, these men preferred to masturbate to pornography. Still others were disturbed that their partners were asking them to participate in sexual acts seen in explicit videos, without regard to whether or not she would find these acts unpleasant or degrading. On the whole, these women reported a strong decline in intimacy and connection with their partners, leaving many to consider breaking off the relationship altogether.[22]

To begin to answer these questions about men's behavior, it's necessary to investigate the experience of viewing pornography. We know men turn on pornography, masturbate to pornography, and then turn it off. But what does that experience feel like? What emotional/psychological processes are at work? I do not want to pretend to answer these questions definitively, but instead I'd like speak to them from my own experience. I claim no scientific status for these observations, but they also are not merely idiosyncratic; I reflect on my life in the context of the experiences of the many men I have spoken to about this over the years, informally as well as in formal interview settings. My claim is not that these observations are true for all men, or that there is a single experience that all men have, but simply that my account is part of the process of understanding how pornography works. And pornography does work—it is an effective and efficient way to spark an erection in a man and create an environment in which he can achieve orgasm relatively quickly. But what does that feel like?

OBJECTIFICATION, OF WOMEN AND OF SELF

Critics of pornography focus on the objectification of women, the way in which women's full humanity is lost and they are reduced to the sum total of their body parts, and the sexual pleasure men get from that. As Andrea Dworkin and others have argued, this is the fundamental process at the core of pornography. Susanne Kappeler writes about this as a basic problem in how men learn to see women:

> The fundamental problem at the root of men's behavior in the world, including sexual assault, rape, wife battering, sexual harassment, keeping women in the home and in unequal opportunities and conditions, treating them as objects for conquest and protection—the root problem behind the reality of men's relations with women, is the way men see women, is Seeing.[23]

I can look back on my life and see how that played out. More important, in the past decade, while conducting my analyses of pornography, I have observed the same process. Even when analyzing pornography through a critical feminist lens, I found that during the time I am viewing the films I am pulled back into a state of mind in which I reflexively evaluate women by their physical appearance. In those studies, I watched the films in concentrated fashion over a period of three or four days, and for some period of weeks after that I noticed the degree to which I was engaging in this kind of reflexive objectification of women all around me. Because of this, I always arranged to do those projects at a time during the summer when I had no teaching duties and could, to the degree possible, have the freedom to spend time alone to decompress from the experience.

My point is that the power of pornography to shape how men view women is, in my experience, so powerful that it can trump the rational process by which I would try to resist it. I found that I could intervene in the process, but it was clear that for some time during and after my viewing, I would objectify first and deconstruct that objectification second. The act of seeing women that way obviously need not lead all men to act in overtly sexist fashion toward women. But it raises more troubling questions: Are there subtle, everyday ways in which men's behavior toward women—in sexual or nonsexual situations—is affected by the training in objectification received in pornography? And is that training so ubiquitous in contemporary culture through media of many kinds, that it becomes the kind of default way of seeing, as Kappeler suggests?

Meanwhile, even as we maintain the primary focus on the way women are objectified in their presentation in pornography—and the consequences of that for all women—it's also crucial to understand the process by which we men objectify ourselves. In my experience, which is also the experience of many men I've talked to over the years, we feel ourselves go emotionally numb when viewing pornography and masturbating, what in common parlance might be called a state of being "checked out" emotionally. To enter into the pornographic world and experience that intense sexual rush, many of us have to turn off some of the emotional reactions that typically are connected to sexual experience with a real person—a sense of the other's humanity, an awareness of being present with another person, the recognition of something outside our own bodies. For me, watching pornography produces a kind of emotional numbness, a part of which is a process of objectifying myself.

In conversation with Meg Baldwin, a feminist law professor at Florida State University who left academic life to run a women's center, I got more insight into this process. Baldwin, who has worked for years with women who are prostituted, said one of the common experiences of those women is coping with the unprovoked rage and violence that johns will direct at them. Baldwin told me that after hearing countless stories about this reaction by men, she concluded the rage was rooted in this self-objectification. She sketched out this process:

> Men typically go to prostitutes to have a sexual experience without having to engage emotionally. Yet when they are in the sexual situation, they sometimes find themselves having those very same emotional reactions they wanted to avoid, simply because our emotional lives cannot be completely controlled. When they feel those things they wanted to suppress, the johns lash out at the most convenient target—the women who they believe caused them to feel what they didn't want to feel.

If Baldwin is right—and, based on my own experience, I believe she is—we could say that men turn women into objects in order to turn ourselves into objects, so that we can split off emotion from body during sex, in search of a sexual experience in which we don't have to feel. But because sex is always more than a physical act, men seeking this split-off state often find themselves having strong emotional reactions, which can get channeled into violence and cruelty.

These observations can help us to fashion an answer to the question I am most often asked by women when they hear descriptions of the sexualized woman-hating of the genre: "Why do men like those things?" Most simply put, men like pornography because it works efficiently to produce erections and orgasms. But the question really is, how can such images produce those erections and orgasms? Why don't men see how the construction of women in pornography doesn't map onto the women they know in the world? I have no definitive answers, but we can start to poke into the corners of men's psyches, places where polite people don't go, to deepen our understanding.

CONTROL

The single most important thing I have learned from analyzing my own history and from the interviews I've conducted is how central the concept of control—of women by men—is to pornography. In my life, that is most clear from the period in which I used pornography the most heavily. It came in my mid-20s after the breakup of a serious relationship with a woman. One reason I found the relationship, and its unraveling, so troublesome was that I was not in control. In most of my intimate relationships before and after, I retained most of the power to make basic decisions about the nature of the relationship. But in that situation, for a variety of reasons, I gave up control to the woman. That left me in a particularly volatile emotional state after the breakup, which I believe made pornography even more attractive.

In pornography, control remains in male hands in two ways. First, the vast majority of sexual scenes in pornographic movies depict sexual encounters in which men are in control, guiding women's actions to produce male pleasure. The images that stay with me from that period are those in which the woman is completely subordinate, performing sexual acts on and for the man. Second, by making female sexuality a commodity, pornography allowed me to control when and where I used it, and therefore used the women in it.

Technology has increased the ability of the viewer to control the sexual experience. The fast-forward button on a videocassette recorder allowed viewers to speed past those portions of the movie that didn't interest them. DVDs offer the same feature, enhanced further by the segmenting of movies by performer or type of sex acts. On many DVDs, one can click to be taken directly to anal penetration, for example.

On an anti-pornography website that includes the reflections of men about their use of pornography, one man explains that this desire for control was a central attraction for him:

> For me, porn is all about CONTROLLING
> HUMAN BEINGS, or I should say the
> ILLUSION of controlling others. That's what
> got me off. I felt so out of control in my life
> and from my childhood, that this was some
> thing I could control (which women I would
> see naked or I could hit the pause button and
> extend a particular image for eternity) for ex
> ample. There is no vulnerability, no risk, and
> therefore—no growth. I think that for me, the
> illusion of controlling women, even in mastur
> batory porn fantasies, was a misguided attempt
> to quell the fear that I have around women. I

know now there are much better ways to deal with these fears.[24]

COMING TO TERMS WITH PORNOGRAPHY'S CONTRADICTIONS

There has been much discussion in both academic and popular literature about the Madonna-whore complex. While there is a specific Freudian use of the term, in general usage it refers to the common way in which men classify women as either Madonna (the good women, mothers and wives, who deserve love and respect) or whore (the bad women whose role is to be used for sex). The message of pornography can reinforce that binary but also can work to undermine it.

Based on the reports not only of men who use pornography but also of the women in their lives, it seems clear that some men use the material with the underlying acceptance of the Madonna-whore distinction—in other words, only whores would do those things, and they exist as a class to do just those kinds of things. Therefore, watching men on-screen do cruel and degrading things to those women raises no concerns. Even if a man wouldn't want those things done to the women in his life, it is acceptable in pornography because those women, whores, are made precisely for that.

But it's also clear that a common message of pornography is that all women are whores by nature; it's intrinsic to being a woman. In pornography, the one thing you know about every woman, no matter what category she is in—mothers and grand-mothers, young women and pregnant women, doctors and nurses, fat and skinny, white and black and all other colors—is that her ultimate value in life is providing sexual pleasure for men. In case the sexual acts alone aren't sufficient, the women in pornography constantly verbalize their status: "I'm a cunt/slut/whore/dirty girl/etc." When women forget to say it, men remind them either with the question "Are you a whore?" or with the command "Say you are a whore."

That's one complex reality: Pornography is one site in the culture that creates whores, that marks some women in the real world—the actual women performing—as subject to being treated that way, distinct from other women. And at the same time, it reinforces the ideology in men's minds that all women are whores.

Another complex reality: Part of the sexual charge of some pornography is that the women are being denigrated and the men watching know that the women don't like it. Part of the appeal of images of women being hurt in a sexual context is that the men watching know it really does hurt the women. But at the same time, the ideology of pornography is that women actually like things that may appear to be denigrating or hurtful, again because it is their nature. So, men's enjoyment of pornography is sometimes based in knowing the woman is in pain, but at the same time being told that it's not really pain because this is how women find their true sexual selves.

As "Buttman," John Stagliano, put it, "pleasure and pain are the same thing, right?"

The men I have known in my life have never had trouble telling the difference between their own pleasure and their own pain. I'm pretty clear about the difference between things that feel good and things that hurt. Pornography tells men that it's different for women. The women in pornography, the whores, clearly like to be treated that way sexually; it's their nature. Most of the women outside pornography, the Madonnas, claim not to like to be treated that way sexually. But maybe, pornography suggests, just maybe those Madonnas are lying. Maybe deep down, all the Madonnas are really whores. Maybe they all like it like that—rough, painful, denigrating.

It's hard not to go from these observations to a simple question: Do men hate women?

The question doesn't suggest that every single man hates every single woman. Instead, we are asking whether there is something in the culture that makes woman-hating inviting. I don't have an answer. But Bill Margold, a longtime pornography performer and producer with a reputation in the industry as a renegade willing to be blunt, does. Margold believes pornography is relatively harmless, but he also acknowledges an ugly side to the business. He doesn't mince words in his analysis of what Stagliano called "a psychology that I don't think is healthy":

> My whole reason for being in the Industry is
> to satisfy the desire of the men in the world
> who basically don't much care for women and
> want to see the men in my Industry getting
> even with the women they couldn't have when
> they were growing up. I strongly believe this,

and the Industry hates me for saying it. ... So we come on a woman's face or somewhat brutalize her sexually: we're getting even for their lost dreams. I believe this. I've heard audiences cheer me when I do something foul on screen. When I've strangled a person or sodomized a person, or brutalized a person, the audience is cheering my action, and then when I've fulfilled my warped desire, the audience applauds.[25]

Pornography producers, consumers, and supporters always talk about how they love women. When accused of producing, consuming, or justifying woman-hating material, they say that pornography is all about the women, that the women are the stars, that pornography celebrates women's sexual power. Here's how one reviewer put it:

But what makes [director John] Leslie's material so hot is what makes Stagliano's work so hot: Sincerity. These guys love women. Women's bodies ignite their imaginations. Their creative impulses are directly linked to their sex drives. From that connection springs hot, raw, real pornography.[26]

I have no doubt that John Stagliano loves specific women in his life. Yet Stagliano, the father of gonzo, also has no general objection to pornography that uses rape scenarios:

I can like a rape scene if I really like the girl and it's done well. The guy is really important in a scene like that, their attitude towards sex. If it's a sexual thing, I am going to like it a lot. If it's just a degradation thing then I'm not going to like it. I'm all about the sex and pretty girls and appreciating them.[27]

Pornography is a genre in which a rape scene need not be a "degradation thing," a genre in which one can appreciate pretty girls having sex in a scene that depicts them as being raped. It's hot, raw, real—common adjectives that the pornography industry loves to use to describe its material. Also increasingly common: dirty, filthy, nasty. These are common terms in a pornography industry that allegedly loves women, terms used by pornography consumers who allegedly love women.

How much more loving can women take?

getting nasty

[ARIANA JOLLEE AND LAURA DAVID]

The first time I heard the word "nasty" used in a sexual context was on the 1971 Black Oak Arkansas album in the song "Hot and Nasty." I was 12 years old and unclear about what band leader Jim Dandy meant when he sang, "Yeah when you ball me, yeah you're hot 'n' nasty." I figured that it had something to do with being sweaty and smelly during sex, about which I knew little.

These days, no 12-year-old would be confused by such lyrics. Today, "hot" and "nasty" are the two of the most common sexual terms tossed around in this culture. "Hot" and "hottie" are used casually in mainstream culture. If you get bored on the internet, for example, you can pickthehottie.com. "Nasty" is the preferred term of endearment in pornography. In nonsexual realms, "nasty" connotes dirty, repellent, offensive, indecent. In pornography, the term means all that and more, which can be wrapped up in one phrase that I heard from a fan at the 2006 AEE in Las Vegas. He told me he liked pornography that was nasty. I asked him what "nasty" meant to him.

"You know, nasty, it's like, really nasty, you know, getting down to it," he said. I told him I was still unclear. "You know, nasty—the things your girlfriend won't do," he said.

I asked him his name. "Mark," he said. Last name? "Forget that—I'm not going to tell you that," he laughed. "You think I want my girlfriend to know I'm looking for the shit she won't do?"

Because different women will do or not do different things, the actual sexual acts that are nasty in this sense will vary from person to person. But whatever nasty is, it marks that which is outside the sexual desire of "normal" women. Nasty, in the pornographic vocabulary, is the sex that sluts want. Nasty is what whores do. Only some women are nasty. Or, more accurately, only some women will act in nasty ways. But because every woman has "an inner slut," every woman really wants to act in nasty ways, and is just held back by social conventions. Deep down, according to the logic of pornography, every woman is a whore, if society would let her be what she is meant to be.

By this logic, the women in pornography—especially the really nasty ones—are the ultimate women. By that standard, Ariana Jollee may well be the perfect woman in a world defined by pornography, someone whose public persona and work on the screen embody the concept of nasty. Her emergence as a popular performer in gonzo pornography coincided with the period I was working on this book, and I wanted to interview her. But such interactions raise complex questions.

In researching the pornography industry, one of the most difficult parts is writing about the women who perform. Women in pornography tend to get treated by men as either objects of desire or objects of ridicule. That is, men see them as things (again, not really people, but things) to be either fucked or made fun of, or both. For example, a pornographic website that focuses on gag-inducing oral sex asks, "Can these fuck toys be any dumber?"[1] That sums up the way men in the pornographic world think about these women.

When pornography performers speak in public they typically repeat a standard script that emphasizes that they have freely chosen this career because of their love of sex and their lack of inhibition. One performer frequently quoted in the press is Nina Hartley, who has written that her career in pornography and stripping was "consciously chosen, as a path to self knowledge, the exploration of sexuality in its many forms."[2] This framing of participation in the sex industry as a feminist act of women taking control of their own lives is common. Whatever the reality of Hartley's description of her own life, this "I am porn performer, hear me roar" framework is a mantra for women in the industry.

While we should listen to and respect those voices, we also know from the testimony of women who leave the sex industry that often they are desperate and unhappy in prostitution and pornography but feel the need to validate it as their choice to avoid thinking of themselves as victims. In a survey of 130 people working as prostitutes, 68 percent were identified as meeting the psychological criteria for a diagnosis of post-traumatic stress disorder, and 88 percent stated that they wanted to leave prostitution and described what they needed in order to escape.[3] As I argued already, the question of choices, and the measure of freedom women have in their choices, is complicated. Respecting the decisions women make does not mean we should ignore the pattern of women speaking quite differently about those decisions later. In a complex world, the way we make sense of our lives is, not surprisingly, full of paradoxes and contradictions.

While knowing all these limitations, several aspects of Jollee's persona and career choices were intriguing, and I was interested in seeing whether it would be possible to speak with her in a way that went beyond the typical script. At the 2006 Adult Entertainment Expo in Las Vegas, I made two appointments to speak with her, but she didn't appear for either. Subsequent phone messages went unanswered. So, I am left with no direct experience with Jollee, only her image on film and her public comments in interviews. In that, however, I think there are moments of insight.

ARIANA JOLLEE: PUBLIC PERSONA

Jollee—who worked in a pornographic film for the first time in 2003 at the age of 20, in *Nasty Girls 30*—performed in hundreds of films in her first few years in the industry and developed a reputation for being willing to do most anything. One reviewer described the "nasty personality of Ariana Jollee" that "makes her a gift for XXX."[4]

When she signed to direct movies for Mayhem, the company proudly announced that the "filthiest girl in all of porn" who was "one of the dirtiest girls ever to hit the adult series" would take the helm of the Young Bung movies. The pornography world was abuzz, the company said, with speculation about "what kind of nasty smut Jollee intends on unleashing into the world."[5] When another company signed her to direct and perform, a commentator noted that both company officials and Jollee concurred that "if ever there was a suitable girl for a company called No Boundaries, it's nasty little Ari."[6]

In an interview with *Adult Video News*, Jollee was described by the publication's editor as a starlet with a "dirty-filthy-nasty-edgy-sex-is-my-entire-reason-for-being" vibe. She reported that she has tried most everything except triple anal:

> AVN: So you really like anal?
>
> Jollee: Yeah.
>
> AVN: What about double vag?
>
> Jollee: No, I don't do double vag. My pussy is so tight. I've done them, but it's painful. No, I don't like it, generally.
>
> AVN: But you like double anal.
>
> Jollee: I cum harder from that than anything else.
>
> AVN: Really?
>
> Jollee: It's so nasty. It feels so good, and it feels fucking wrong on top of it.

Jollee also said she is angered by people who criticize these types of sexual performances as being wrong or too nasty:

> I love two dicks in my fucking ass. I did double anal the other day, and I wasn't even booked for it. I've done that on more than one occasion. I did double anal with Cheyne Collins and Tyce Bune, because they wanted to bang me in the ass together. And I didn't even get paid to do double anal. I didn't want to. It's a sex act. You're filming a sex act. It [the criticism] shouldn't be directed at sex. Let it be boy/girl, or double anal, or fucking a giant orgy or some 20 million-man gangbang. It's a sex act. Let it be the way it is.[7]

When my coworkers on the documentary film crew interviewed Jollee at the AEE in Las Vegas in 2005, she spoke in a fashion typical of pornography performers, celebrating her work as an expression of who she really is:

> I'm just a filthy pervert who, I don't know, doing what I love. ... I can get off on people slapping me across the face or beating me up because I

want it. It's a fantasy. So it's not necessarily like normal, [but] it's not degradation. We're just celebrating our bodies and being erotic, natural human beings.

Jollee told the interviewer that when she first saw pornography she thought, "I want to do it and I want to get paid for it." She said that she enjoyed all the acts she engages in on-screen, though she hints that to enjoy some things it takes a force of will:

Well, double anal—it's filthy and wrong and disgusting. It's so fucking good. So, it's good. It's real good. ... If you want it bad enough, it won't be painful. You just have to want it, that's all. ... Double penetration isn't painful at all. It's one of the best feelings in the world. It's filthy and if you believe it feels good, it will always feel good, so just give it a try.

When an interviewer for a pornography-related website interviewed her in 2004, he asked whether it was possible for a pornography performer to have a private life. Jollee said:

There's parts of me that I don't let people see. I'm very particular about who I let close to me and there's not many. It's very hard to get there. Maybe one or two people. But I do give a lot to a lot of people. That's one of my problems. I give a lot. In everything I do. And when you don't get it back, it's very disappointing. There's parts of me no one knows about. But it's nice to keep the mystery, and keep people guessing and shock them. Oh my God, she reads! You know what I mean? She just cooked the meanest steak I ever had in my life. I write music. No one knows that. I've always been very creative.[8]

ARIANA JOLLEE: SCREEN PERSONA

Jollee performed in JM Productions' 2005 release *Swirlies*. The film is typical gonzo sex with a gimmick: At the end of each scene, the man dunks the woman's head in a toilet and flushes.

As the company puts it, "Every whore gets the swirlies treatment. Fuck her, then flush her."

In her scene with the male performer Jenner, Jollee comes to his door to complain that his little brother had given her little brother a swirlie at school. This setup lasts under a minute before the sex acts, which include oral, vaginal, and anal penetration in the typical positions that give the camera as much access as possible to the performers' genitals. The oral penetration includes gag-inducing deep penetration, and the anal penetration is in several different positions. After ejaculating on her face, Jenner takes her to the bathroom for a swirlie.

Here is a sample of the words Jollee speaks in the movie during sex:

> "Shove it up my fucking ass. ... fuck that fucking tight little motherfucking asshole. Ah, that's so fucking good."
>
> "Fuck that motherfucking filthy asshole motherfucker. Fucking amazing. So fucking amazing. Fucking fuck me motherfucker."
>
> "Fucking cock in that little asshole. That fucking dick in my fucking tight little filthy motherfucking asshole."
>
> "Fucking love it. Fucking love it."
>
> "Fuck motherfucker is fucking me. Ride that fucking cock, huh."
>
> "Fucking nice hard cock in fucking tight little ass. Fuck me like a fucking little puppy, huh. Little puppy dog, huh. Fuck me with that fucking cock so hard. So fucking hard shoot your fucking hot cum all over my pretty little motherfucking face like a dirty little filthy motherfucking whore."

In the middle of the scene, Jenner—who has been mostly silent, as men often are in pornography—finally speaks up, finally says, "Yeah, fuck yeah, that's it, talk fucking dirty like a real fucking whore."

Jollee's response sums up her on-screen persona: "Fucking dirty. I'm a filthy little fucking whore."

In the hundreds of films Jollee has made, she is often just one female performer among many. But she was the only woman in *65 Guy Cream Pie*, a gangbang film produced in 2004 by Devil's Film featuring her with 65 men.

In an interview conducted before the filming, which is included in the DVD extras, Jollee says she performed in a 21-man gangbang on her 21st birthday and was looking forward to doing this 50-man event (which eventually became 65 on the set). "Cream pie" is a pornographic term that refers to men ejaculating in the woman's vagina or anus, rather than ejaculating onto her body or into her mouth.

"Stuff like this is meant for me," she says. "I like going wild and crazy." In the interview, she talks about how she expects to be sexually voracious during filming, but then reflects: "Maybe they'll fuck me up. Maybe they'll really like teach me a lesson. Maybe I'm not as insatiable as I think I am." She explains that she likely will "look like shit" when it's over but will be "well fucked." The interviewer asks what shape her vagina and anus will be in after. She talks about her body parts in the third person: "They can take it. They want it. They like it. They go back to size after. Pussy's tight. She always goes back to size."

In that interview she also talks about her private life. She says that prior to her on-screen gangbangs, in her personal life she had once had sex with 12 men on a fire truck. She won't say how old she was at the time, but her remarks suggest she was a teenager. About that experience, she says: "It was so good. I will thank that man who took me there every day for the rest of my life. I still talk to him; he's a really good friend of mine. He's a pervert but I love perverts. I like free people."

At this point, her pornographic manner fades for a quiet moment, and her face is hard to read. Her ambiguous expression suggests that there could be more to the story, that the day on the fire truck was something more complicated, that maybe such an experience for a teenager on a fire truck was not simply the product of her sexual desire. Or maybe the story is invented, all part of the performance for the pornography consumer. The only thing we know for sure is that viewers won't get the full story on this DVD. After that moment, Jollee quickly goes back into the pornography performer, saying, "I hope everyone gets off. I plan on cumming."

In the six hours of filming,[9] Ariana has oral sex, vaginal sex, anal sex, DP sex, and double anal sex with 65 men. They ejaculate onto her body and inside her body. She collects their semen in a cup and drinks it at several points in the film. Yet after several hours of having sex with 65 men, Jollee retains a strange ability to be what appears to be emotionally present. One of the men, who seems to have little experience with sex, takes his turn and is awkward. Jollee is understanding, even tender, with him in the middle of this sexual circus. "You going to cum for me?" she asks, and they begin vaginal intercourse in the missionary position. She tries to guide him. "If you're going to fuck, fuck the right way. Come on, fuck like you fuck at home," she says. She then looks to the camera operators and director, apparently to check to make sure the scene is acceptable to them, and then turns back to the man. With as much compassion as is possible in such a setting, she encourages him to slow down. "Baby, relax. Slow down. Slow. Slow. Fuck for real," Jollee says. She points his face toward her, to get him to look at her, but he refuses to meet her gaze and looks back down at her vagina, giggling out of apparent nervousness. She looks over at the other men and shrugs, as if to say, "I tried." It's an odd moment of attempted intimacy, but only a moment. Jollee quickly returns to regular porn talk: "Cum for me motherfucker."

When it's all over, Jollee goes into a bathroom, which viewers can see on the behind-the-scenes feature of the DVD. After six hours and 65 men, as she roams the bathroom looking for the appropriate cloth to wipe herself off with, Jollee talks to the man operating the camera:

> Jollee: Oh my God, wow. You ever see anything like that? What did you think?
>
> Cameraman: I think you wore those guys out.
>
> Jollee: They wore me out. I won't fucking deny that. Look at me. I'm about to pass out.
>
> [*She pauses briefly and then looks at the man with the camera, with a very vulnerable expression.*]
>
> Jollee: Good gangbang?
>
> Cameraman: Yes, it was intense. Very good.
>
> Jollee: Thank you. I tried.

This nastiest of the filthy women in pornography, this woman about to turn 22 years old, turns to a man who makes his living in the pornography industry and asks for his approval, asking if her sex with 65 men was a "good gangbang." The questions—not her question, but larger questions that her comment suggests—hang in the air, unaddressed. What kind of world is this, in which a 21-year-old woman has sex with 65 men in one day to produce a movie that thousands of other men will masturbate to for years to come? What kind of world is this, in which that young woman can seek validation through men's approval of her extreme sexual performance? What kind of world is this, in which asking those simple questions can get one labeled a prude?

Not surprisingly, *65 Guy Cream Pie* at that point doesn't take up those questions. Instead, Jollee goes back into her upbeat character, asking the man, "Are you having fun with the camera?"

What should a viewer make of all this—of the fire truck, the tenderness toward the man in bed, and the exchange in the bathroom after the gangbang? What conclusions should we draw about Ariana Jollee? From this limited information, it would be folly to claim to know anything. The small hints that come out during the film or in the DVD extras are nothing but hints, too subtle for the pornographers to even care to edit out. Nothing is clear; there's nothing a viewer can conclude for certain. If someone were to ask me, "Who is Ariana Jollee?" I would be hard pressed to offer much of an answer.

One thing we can know for sure is that this young woman's real name is not Ariana Jollee. Various online sources report that her real name is Laura David.[10]

So, maybe the important question isn't "Who is Ariana Jollee?" Maybe the right question is "Who is Laura David?"

not-masculinity

where we need to go

MEN WILL BE MEN

In 2005 I was invited to speak on pornography to a conference on college men at St. John's University, an all-male Catholic college in central Minnesota run by a Benedictine monastery. I didn't hesitate to accept, in part because I'm eager to talk to any and all men about these issues, and also because I had worked at that campus 20 years earlier and was glad to have a chance to visit.

When I served there as the news director from 1983–84, the university was at the beginning stages of a transition around gender and sex issues. At that time, it was expanding its coop-erative relationship with a nearby all-female school, the College of St. Benedict, run by a Benedictine convent. Reflecting the gender politics of the Catholic church, the men of St. John's assumed that they belonged in a position of dominance, and during my time there it led to more than a few tense moments in joint planning meetings. Although at that time I had yet to read feminist writing or give much thought to questions about gender and power, even as a naïve young professional man I could see that my male colleagues, especially the older ones, were not comfortable with any notion that St. John's and St. Ben's were—or ever could be—on equal footing. Some of the monks and lay faculty, male and female, were pushing for such equality, but there also was considerable resistance.

Here's an illustrative example about a relatively small issue: As the two schools produced more joint brochures, the staff at St. Ben's requested that collectively produced material use the term "first-year students" instead of "freshmen." In their separate publications, St. Ben's had made that switch, for the obvious reason that there are no "men" students, "fresh" or otherwise, on that campus. In a meeting with my counterpart at the women's college, I said I couldn't see why such a policy for joint publications would be a problem and that I would inform my colleagues of the change. I was wrong. When I got back to St. John's, I found that, indeed, many of my fellow staff members, all men, saw lots of problems: "Freshman" is the traditional term. And besides, everyone understands it's gender neutral. And "first-year students" is clumsy. And the St. Ben's staff members are too sensitive about this kind of thing.

And on it went, with reasons I've long since forgotten trotted out to explain why this minor change that would cost nothing was unacceptable. But the real reason was never spoken: Girls don't get to tell boys what to do. More specifically, the women of St. Ben's don't tell the men of St. John's what to do. The struggle wasn't over the word, of course; it was about power. Everyone at St. John's knew that the old days of overt male dominance were over, but that didn't mean they had accepted a relationship of equality. While the two schools retained distinct identities, with residential facilities and some non-academic activities separate, the academic programs of the two schools had been merged (students from both campuses took the same classes). The schools' rhetoric was of a cooperative relationship based on equality.

Some of the men of St. John's grudgingly accepted the rhetoric but couldn't really come to terms with the notion of equality. Everyone was polite, but the strains were impossible to miss. The result was embarrassingly juvenile arguments about "freshman" in which the men revealed what really annoyed them: The women seemed to really believe the equality rhetoric and sometimes pressed for it.

Fast-forward 20 years, to the Second Annual Conference on the College Male. I was happy to hear that the St. John's administration had given full support to the conference and its explicitly pro-feminist agenda, and I was curious about what might have changed on campus. Although it wasn't clear to me what specific problems college men experience (as opposed to the problems they cause) or why a conference on them was necessary, I went into the event open-minded and hopeful that the organizers were recognizing the importance of feminism to men. I was heartened that they wanted me to speak about pornography, aware of the radical feminist analysis in which my work was based.

The first hint that my politics would be out of place was the self-congratulatory tone of the opening evening, as the men involved seemed to spend most of the time explaining why the conference was so important. The keynote speaker, a man whose work is rooted in feminism, made important points, but his talk had that same tone. Although everyone spoke of the need for men to be critically self-reflective about male power and privilege, the underlying message I took away was "we are the good guys, the men who have transcended sexism."

In part because of my reaction to that tone, my talk the next day began in blunt terms:

> There has been much talk at this conference about the need for men to love each other and be willing to speak openly about that love. That is important; we need to be able to get beyond the all-too-common male tendency to mute or deform our emotions, a tendency that is destructive not only to ourselves but to those around us. Many this weekend have spoken about our need to nurture each other, and that's important, too. But it's also crucial to remember that loving one another means challenging ourselves as well.
>
> That's what I would like to do today, to challenge us—in harsh language—on men's use of pornography. In an unjust world, those of us with privilege must be harsh on ourselves, out of love.
>
> This challenge is: Can we be more than just johns?

The jocular mood of the conference evaporated quickly. I critiqued the idea that one could be for gender justice and use pornography, buy women in prostitution, or go to strip bars. Such talk in groups of men (even pro-feminist men) is always uncomfortable, for the obvious reason that many of the men in the room continue to patronize the sexual-exploitation industries and don't want to be confronted. And for those who had stopped those practices, I suggested our work, personal and collective, wasn't over:

> The way out of being a john is political. The way out is feminism. I don't mean feminism as a superficial exercise in identifying a few "women's issues" that men can help with. I mean feminism as an avenue into what Karl Marx called "the ruthless criticism of the existing order, ruthless in that it will shrink neither from its own discoveries, nor from conflict with the powers that be."
>
> We need to engage in some ruthless criticism. Let's start not just with pornography, but with sex more generally. One of those discoveries, I think, is not only that men often are johns, but that the way in which johns use women sexually is a window into other aspects of our sexual and intimate lives as well. For many men, sex is often a place where we both display and reinforce our power over women. By that, I don't mean that all men at all times use sex that way, but that a pattern of such relationships is readily visible in this society. Women deal with it every day, and at some level most men understand it.
>
> We can see that pornography not only raises issues about the buying and selling of women, but—if we can remain ruthless and not shrink from our own discoveries—about sex in general, about the way in which men and women in this culture are commonly trained to be sexual. It's not just about pimps and johns and the women prostituted. It's about men and women, and sex and power. If throughout this discussion you have been thinking, "Well, that's not me—I never pay for it," don't be so sure. It's not just about who pays for it and who doesn't. It's about the fundamental nature of the relation-

ship between men and women, and how that plays out in sex and intimacy.

Clunk.

My words dropped like a stone in water. Typically after talks on this subject, there are many people who want to engage me, either to express agreement or to explain why they think I'm crazy. The subject tends to spark lively debate, but not after this talk. The man who had invited me politely thanked me for coming, and one man from the audience came up to say he thought the challenge was important. The rest of the audience hit the doors quickly. Only two or three men approached me over the next day that I remained at the conference.

The lack of engagement could be because I'm an unpleasant person. But even if that's true, any lack of interpersonal skills on my part hasn't stopped people from haranguing me in the past. Instead, I think the explanation is more likely that I had ruined their party. They had planned a conference on the college male from this "new" paradigm of a reconstituted masculinity. I suggested that we men—all of us, me and them—had a lot more work to do before we started celebrating anything, and that the work required that we leave masculinity behind, not reconstruct it. My final words to them were:

> We live in a time of sexual crisis. That makes life difficult, but it also creates a space for invention and creativity. That is what drew me to feminism, to the possibility of a different way of understanding the world and myself, the possibility of escaping the masculinity trap set for me, that chance to become something more than a man, more than just a john—to become a human being.

We need to puzzle through what that might mean, for men to become human beings.

SEX: DIFFERENCES AND SIMILARITIES

After a one-hour radio debate with me and a review of some of my writing, the editor of *Hustler* magazine offered this diagnosis: "I'd submit that Jensen is a deeply disturbed individual at war with his own masculinity."[1]

Whether or not I'm disturbed, deeply or otherwise, I will leave to the judgment of others, but editor Bruce David was wrong to suggest I'm at war with *my* masculinity. If I'm at war, it's with the culture's conception of masculinity and, beyond that, with the notion of masculinity itself. But David was right in asserting that I am:

> not only against pornography; he is against masculinity as well. He believes the very attributes of maleness need to be redefined. He doesn't want you to watch football or play it either. He thinks it makes men too aggressive. He thinks porn and sports are at least partly responsible for child and spousal abuse.

That's a little muddled, but he gets some things right. I don't think sports are responsible for child and spousal abuse, but I do think that the dominant conception of masculinity that plays out so often in sports is rooted in the same conception of masculinity that leads to abuse. I think our task is to face the difficult truths about men's behavior and the notions of masculinity that underlie that behavior, to engage in some ruthless criticism, willing to face the implications—personal and societal—of what we learn.

There is a growing awareness throughout the culture that such criticism is necessary, that the traits commonly associated with masculinity—competition, aggression, domination, and repression of emotion—are not only linked to men's violence against others but are toxic for men themselves. One strategy is to redefine masculinity based on other values. While successful in producing behavior change in some situations with some men, it is a dangerous move because it reinforces notions that the physical differences between men and women translate into social differences. Our goal should be not to redefine masculinity, but to abolish it. Attempts to identify and valorize alternative masculine traits add to, rather that detract from, men's capacity to move away from a position of domination. Any short-term efforts to redefine masculinity to lower levels of violence must go forward with a consciousness about the inherent danger of the category itself.

To make the case against masculinity, a comparison to racial categories is helpful. Unlike sex categories, racial categories are arbitrary. While based on observable physical differences (that is, my European American/white skin is noticeably lighter than the skin of someone in the racial category of African American/black),[2] the division of people into racial categories is not required for human survival or flourishing, nor is it based on any philosophical principle or biological law. That is, we could easily imagine living with no concept of racial distinctions among humans. The observable physical differences would remain, but skin color would be no more relevant for creating categories than the size of one's ears, for example. People have different-sized ears, and we could arbitrarily divide the world into the large-eared vs. small-eared, but we don't. Whatever small genetic differences between humans it turns out there might be that are rooted in the region of origin of one's ancestors (and, hence, have some connection to what we call "race"), those aren't the basis for a meaningful biological concept of race. Race, then, is a social construct, based on real physical differences, but differences that have meaning only because of a social process.

Sex categories are different. To reproduce, humans must take note of the physical difference between males and females. If men were to think they had an equal chance of producing a child through sexual intercourse with another man or a woman, the species would be in trouble. This is not an argument that sexuality has no function other than reproduction, a position that often leads to heterosexist assumptions and anti-lesbian/gay politics, bur rather a simple observation about material realities. For humans to mark reproductive differences—to see male and female as distinctively different—is inevitable; the process is not arbitrary.

So, we can imagine a world with no race categories, but it would be impossible—outside of science fiction—to construct a world without sex categories. Our eventual goal, then, should be to eliminate the concept of race, though of course in the short term we must retain the categories to deal with the pernicious effects of the social/political realities of white supremacy and racism.

To argue that we should reject masculinity is not to argue that we can eliminate the category of sex. Such an argument does not require us to ignore the obvious physical differences between males and females—e.g., average body size, hormones, reproductive organs. Given those relatively easy-to-identify physical differences, it's likely there are other differences rooted in our biology that we don't yet understand. So, the fact that men and women have different plumbing and wiring is uncontroversial, but making claims about deeper intellectual and/or emotional and/or spiritual differences between males and females based on those physical differences—let alone claims about what we should or shouldn't do in response to such differences—should be quite controversial.

I approach this issue from a cautious position in intellectual terms, one that not only acknowledges the extremely limited amount of knowledge we have at the moment but also recognizes that we humans do not have the intellectual ability to allow us to say much of anything in the near future. At our current level of understanding, with the tools we have available to us, it's unlikely we'll know much more anytime soon about these questions concerning potential intellectual/emotional/spiritual differences. In other words, this is one of the many questions about a complex world in which we are fundamentally ignorant—what we don't know overwhelms what we do know. The latest discoveries from neuroscience, as impressive as they are, simply add a few more drops to the bucket of human knowledge that is a long way from filled.

We know that males and females are more alike in biological terms than different. We don't know how much of a difference those differences make in terms of the intellectual/emotional/spiritual processes, nor do we know much about how malleable any differences that do exist might be. Certainly the existence of patriarchy indicates the differences are there; systems rooted in men's oppression of women obviously wouldn't have arisen without some biological differences that made a difference. But that fact says nothing about our ability to construct a society that mitigates the effects of such differences; it's certainly plausible that we have the capacity to overcome whatever physical differences led to patriarchal societies.

Simply put: In any human population, there is considerable individual variation. While there's no doubt that a large part of our behavior is rooted in our DNA, there's also no doubt that how our genetic endowment plays out in the world is highly influenced by culture. Beyond that, it's difficult to say much with any certainty. It's true that only women can bear children and breastfeed. Not all women do that, of course, but only women can. That fact likely has some bearing on aspects of men's and women's personalities. But we don't know much about what the effect is, and it's not likely we ever will know much.

At the moment, the culture seems obsessed with gender differences, in the context of a recurring intellectual fad (called "evolutionary psychology" this time around, and "sociobiology" in a previous incarnation) that wants to explain all complex behaviors as simple evolutionary adaptations—if a pattern of human behavior exists, it must be because it's an adaptation in some ways. In the long run, that's true. But in the short term— the arena in which we have to evaluate and analyze—it's hardly a convincing argument to say, "Look at how men and women behave differently; it must be because men and women are fundamentally different" when a system of power (patriarchy) has been creating social differences between men and women for centuries. It may be that in the long run, patriarchy is not a successful adaptation in evolutionary terms and will lead to the extinction of the species. As we look around the world at the threats to sustainable life rooted in patriarchal societies, that's not only plausible but increasingly hard to deny. That suggests a rejection of patriarchy, which makes possible long-term human survival, may well be a successful adaptation in evolutionary terms.

No matter what the future holds, we should be skeptical of grand claims made about the meaning of those perceived differences between men and women, given the pernicious effects of patriarchy and its relentless devaluing of things female. In the ongoing cultural conversation, these issues often reduce to claims that some aspect of human behavior is "natural." At one level, this is a true, but empty, statement. If human beings can do something, by definition it means that the behavior is within our nature to do and is, therefore, in some sense natural. We all have within us, as part of our nature, the ability to engage in a range of behaviors. We have the capacity to be kind and loving to friends and family, and then turn around and torture them. We have the capacity to love our children and to beat them to death. All of these activities are natural in this basic sense, and they happen frequently enough that they cannot be written off as the aberrant behavior of a limited part of the population that is sociopathic.

But most of the time, when people assert that a behavior is "natural," they are making a much more extensive claim; they are asserting or implying that the behavior is either morally desirable or, if not desirable, extremely difficult to change. Some argue that such changes are so difficult that the individual and/or social "costs" of trying outweigh any likely benefit, though such claims are usually being made by just those people whose privilege is being threatened. Is it surprising that such people are quick to assert the status quo is natural?

Men's control of women is seen by many as natural. It is natural, of course, at the level of the tautology I just described— "if it exists, it's natural." But is it morally desirable? Or, if not, is it simply a fact of life that can't be changed? I would answer "no" to both. At this point, we have to leave discussions of what is clearly biological and talk about how societies make sense of male and female.

REDEFINING OR ELIMINATING MASCULINITY?

How a society understands the differences and similarities between males and females, and then goes on to impose those understandings on people, is a social and political question. The process by which those questions are answered is collective and reflects the distribution of power in society. We have choices, and the choices we have made in the past have to change if we are to make good on the principles of justice that most of us claim to hold. For those committed to gender justice, that means we have a choice between working to redefine masculinity away from the dominant conception that leads to negative consequences such as sexual assault, or working to eliminate the concept of masculinity altogether. After many years of struggling with the former, I have in recent years shifted to the latter project.

A large part of the reason for that shift is, ironically, watching feminist men play out the same old King of the Hill games while trying to contribute to gender justice. For example, for several years I observed two well-known pro-feminist writers jockey for dominance in various forums. Their disagreements were substantive, and such disagreements are important to air, but the style in which their debate emerged was a slightly more polite version of what is sometimes called "dick waving," ritual behavior aimed at establishing dominance. Watching that play out was a painful reminder that I am prone to similar behavior; it's easy for a man to claim to resist the dominant conception of masculinity, to be successful at that resistance in various ways, and yet still revert to the pursuit of dominance in more subtle ways. I have also watched a pro-feminist man who does excellent anti-violence work in public speak in private in the same arrogant language of dominance with which I was so familiar from the locker room and other all-male spaces. That was another cautionary lesson for me, about how easy it is to fall into the masculinity trap. More often than I would like to admit, I catch myself—or am caught by others—speaking in similar fashion.

These observations, and my own continuing struggles, forced me to ask: Should the goal simply be to reconstruct a kinder-and-gentler masculinity? If so, how do we keep ourselves from backsliding into the dominant conception of masculinity that surrounds us in a patriarchal world? Does that desire to find some new way to "be a man" and hold on to masculinity reveal a deep attachment to a position of dominance? Is that backsliding inevitable so long as we hold on to the idea of masculinity? Obviously the act of renouncing masculinity doesn't magically change behavior. But the fact that most men react with reflexive hostility to the idea indicates to me that it's a good place to start the conversation; if men are that afraid of moving beyond masculinity, there's something there to investigate further.

The first step is simply to ask why men feel such a deep investment in the notion of masculinity, no matter how the term is defined. What are we afraid of losing? I think the answer is simple enough. Masculinity—any notion of masculinity—provides men with a way to be assured that they are not, and never will be, a woman. Masculinity guarantees a man that no matter what happens to him in the world, he is not-woman. In any culture that hates women, such a guarantee is bound to feel good, even for pro-feminist men who wouldn't ever dare say such a thing out loud. That guarantee is also bound to keep us from fully confronting that woman-hating and experiencing our full humanity.

So, I cannot escape a simple conclusion: If men are going to be full human beings, we first have to stop being men.[3]

Proposing a strategy of abolishing masculinity doesn't generate controversy in the United States today—for the simple reason that to most people the idea is unintelligible. In a society in which biological sex differences are believed to lead to significant and immutable psychological gender differences, the project of eliminating masculinity literally doesn't make sense to many people. But it is a rather simple and elegant argument.

Let's set the idea in a concrete situation. After 9/11, one of the participants on a pro-feminist e-mail list suggested that the actions of men on that tragic day could help us rethink masculinity. The writer suggested that the fact that male firefighters raced into burning buildings, risking and sometimes sacrificing their lives to save others, could remind us that masculinity can encompass a kind of strength that is rooted in caring and sacrifice instead of power and dominance. Could this not be a space in which we could redefine masculinity?

My response was simple: Of course men often exhibit such strength, just as do women. So, what might make these distinctly masculine characteristics? Are they not simply human characteristics? Is there any characteristic we might label "masculine" that is present in men to some significantly greater degree that makes it clearly more intrinsic to male humans than female humans and, therefore, deserves to be called masculine? I cannot identify any, nor can anyone else. Again, there are biological differences between men and women, but can we with any confidence link biology to any set of psychological or moral traits?

It is important to talk about different patterns of men's and women's behavior. We identify men's tendencies toward competition, domination, and violence because we see these distinct patterns of behavior; men are more prone to such behavior in our culture. Whatever the biological roots of such behaviors might be (and, again, we don't have the tools to answer that question with any certainty), we easily can observe and analyze the ways in which men are socialized to behave in those ways, and we can set a goal of changing those destructive behaviors by changing the socialization.

That kind of analysis is very different than arguing that admirable human qualities present in both men and women should be identified in any way as primarily the domain of one gender. To assign them to a gender is misguided, and demeaning to the gender that is then assumed not to possess them to the same degree. Asserting that "strength and courage are masculine traits"—even if we acknowledge that women can be strong and courageous, too—can only lead to the conclusion that women are not as strong or courageous. Otherwise, would we not just identify them as human traits? To say "strength and courage are masculine traits," then, implicitly supports sexist assumptions.

The only argument I can imagine for this attempt to redefine masculinity is a strategic one—that as an interim strategy we should try to give men new ways to think about masculinity that can lead them away from the toxic and dangerous dominant conception. I certainly understand the appeal, but I am always wary of strategies that involve an underlying premise that is illogical.

"REAL" MEN AND THEIR STRENGTH

This abolitionist approach is a minority position not only in the wider culture but in the anti-violence movement itself. Many activists working to reduce—and, we hope, eventually eliminate—rape, battery, and child sexual assault endorse and employ the strategy of redefining masculinity. One common slogan is "real men don't rape."[4] The idea that one can be a man and not engage in such violence is clear and easy to communicate, yet it entrenches a commitment to masculinity by invoking the idea that there is a way to be a real man, that there is something about men, in psychological or moral terms, that is distinctive from women. No matter what one is claiming that real men do—whether it is not eating quiche[5] or not beating women—the claim depends on accepting the idea that there is a set of actions or ways of being, flowing from a set of traits, that defines men. Such a claim is based on a claim that masculinity is a biological, rather than a social, reality.

Another public-education campaign shows men asserting that "my strength is not for hurting."[6] Again, the strategy of giving men a way to think of themselves as powerful in a fashion that does not have to lead to violence is a reasonable short-term strategy. But it also represents a commitment to masculinity-as-dominance, overtly linking masculinity and strength. There is no explicit statement that women are not strong, but a clear suggestion that men are stronger. Men are, on average, bigger than women, and one notion of strength is correlated with size. But this image and slogan carries with it far more than an observation about comparative muscle mass. It buys into a notion of gender that identifies men not only as strong but as naturally in control as a result of that strength.

Whatever the goals of those who created these messages, such attempts to reformulate masculinity do not challenge men's sense of themselves as dominant. They do not disrupt men's belief in their natural role as being in charge. If we could know that such campaigns are effective at reducing men's violence, their use could be defended. But we should recognize that these tactics make the long-term goal of eliminating masculinity more difficult.

In Shared Hope International's "The Defenders" campaign, launched in 2006 to end men's patronage of the sexual-exploitation industries that target children, we see another potential problem in these strategies. Although the religious language is muted, the campaign is rooted in a conservative Christian perspective that implicitly rejects feminism's critique of male dominance. From this perspective, male dominance is a positive force, but one that must be used to protect rather than exploit children.

At first glance it may seem hard to argue with this, no matter what one's political grounding. If one wants to reduce men's violence against children, having men publicly state their opposition to "the sexual exploitation of children, using pornography, and buying sex" is to be celebrated. But the underlying conception of masculinity is troubling. Why should men do this? Because such behavior "is not something real men will tolerate." Why not? Because "real men" are defenders, "men who take seriously our role to be protectors and providers."

Men provide. Men protect. Men defend. The campaign speaks only of men protecting children, which raises obvious questions: Where are the adult women in all of this? Shouldn't they be protecting children, too? Can they be defenders? Or do they need protection as well?

Another obvious question: Who put men in charge?

Whether one believes it was God or nature that made men the natural protectors, the result is the same: Patriarchy. And inevitably in patriarchy, women and children suffer. If men are to protect women and children, men must have the power to protect. As one defender of this conception of masculinity put it in a widely discussed book, "How can I protect you properly if I can't tell you what to do?"[7] Real men protect, which means real men must have the power to protect, which means real men must have the right to tell women what to do.

All this talk is a cover for a simple, ugly fact: Women and children don't need to be protected *by* men—they need to be protected *from* men. This talk of protection should be seen for what it is: A protection racket. One man or group of men promises to protect women and children from other men. And to do that, these good men must have the power to protect, which means the power to control.[8]

If men, real or otherwise, truly wanted to help end violence and exploitation, there is an obvious path: Join with women in women-led campaigns to end the abuses perpetrated by men. If men are the ones committing the vast majority of violence against women and children, perhaps it is best if we give women a shot at leadership in campaigns to end the violence.

There's a name for that: Feminism. Men can find their place in a feminist movement to end men's violence; there are plenty of organizations eager to welcome men into the struggle. But there's one problem: In a feminist organization, there is no King of the Hill. Feminist organizations sometimes struggle with women vying to be Queen of the Hill, though the groups with which I have been involved have been largely successful at avoiding that dynamic. The goal of feminism, as I was taught it and have tried to practice it, is not the power-over that real men seek, but power-with—power that is created and expanded by collaborative efforts, not seized and controlled by leadership. Those are lofty goals that are, sadly, often not met. But it is crucial that the goal is there, that the path to another understanding of oneself and one's role in the world is available to male humans.

FEMININITY

So far I have purposefully said nothing about femininity, the corresponding belief that there is something in the nature of female humans that allows us to identify traits that are specific to them as a result of biology. I have not critiqued the way in which female humans become, in social terms, women.

As a man, I understand my obligation to be first to focus on the unjust exercise of power by men that flows from a particular conception of masculinity, and the idea of masculinity more generally. Logically, an end to masculinity would also mean an end to femininity, to treating certain states of mind, emotions, and behaviors as intrinsic to female humans. Many of my radical feminist female friends and allies agree with that goal. Not all women concur. Here I will attempt neither to describe nor to evaluate femininity, but simply to observe that in a world without conceptions of masculinity rooted in biology (or theological imperatives), it's difficult to imagine how conceptions of femininity could exist; losing one half of a binary usually means the other half will fade as well. Again, to argue this is not to ignore the material differences between male and female humans, but instead to offer proposals on how to understand those differences.

WHAT WOULD BE LEFT?

The most interesting aspect of this issue is the question people often ask when presented with the abolitionist idea: Well, if males aren't men, what would they be? The simple answer—that they would be human beings—seems to puzzle many people. When I speak of these ideas, men often assume I want to eliminate all behaviors that traditionally are associated with masculinity, that I want to create a world in which no man ever plays football. That is not the case. Eliminating the concept of masculinity would not destroy the activity of throwing and running with a ball under a set of rules. If we left behind the concept of masculinity, undoubtedly the way people play football would change; I suspect it would be a much less violent game, for example, and I would count that as a good thing.

The concern for how we male humans could understand ourselves in a world without masculinity, without a series of assumptions we could make about what it means to be a man, is rooted in a fear of the unknown. Even though many men find the demands of masculinity stressful, even debilitating at times, the masculinity rituals are familiar and can be reassuring, even when they are the source of pain. The call to go beyond masculinity to a new humanity asks people to imagine something for which we have no model. It is frightening, but like most things that spark fear it also opens up the possibility of finding something deeper, richer, and more satisfying. It demands of us imagination and an acceptance of walking into unknown territory. Such a journey indeed is frightening, but exhilarating at the same time.

One place to start that journey is the core of sex and gender: Sexuality.

conclusion

pornography

People talk a lot about sex. Some people talk about the kind of sex they like, about how much they want to do it and with whom. Other people talk about how those people are having too much sex or sex with the wrong people, or simply are talking too much about these things they shouldn't want and shouldn't be doing.

Yet with all this talk, there's very little serious discussion in this culture of a simple question: What is sex for? What is— what should be—the function of sex in the lives of humans in the 21st century? Of all of the ways in which people might possibly understand and use sexuality in their lives, which are most consistent with human flourishing? Which are most consistent with a just and sustainable society? In a world with more easily available birth control and a greater (though far from complete) acceptance of lesbian and gay sexuality, the question should attract even more attention, as the amount of sexual activity that is not even potentially connected to reproduction has expanded dramatically.

At various times and places in this society, especially within certain religious traditions, an answer to the question "what is sex for?" has been imposed on people in ways that are not just arbitrary and constraining, but sometimes stunningly inhumane. Take the simple question of masturbation. How many children who have explored their own sexuality through masturbation have been told they are engaged in sinful behavior? What kind of shame do those children carry and for how long? For how many of those children will those lessons linger into adulthood and hinder the development of a healthy relationship with one's own body and healthy intimacy with another?

In patriarchal, heterosexist cultures, these kinds of authoritarian dictates about sex have left scars of varying depth on many people, including me. Given that history, it's not surprising that many people want to opt out of the question and—either implicitly or explicitly—proceed as if there can be no answer, because any answer will constrain someone and be open to misuse by others. It's true that any way we collectively offer answers about "what sex is for," it will place someone's sexual practices outside the norm, no matter how expansive and inclusive the answer. But it's crucial to recognize that to reject the question also has consequences.

We should start with the recognition that precisely because they are powerful experiences, intimacy and sex are never risk free. Even in a homogenous world in which everyone agreed on the role of sex, it's likely that in the course of intimacy, people would at times experience hurt and rejection, disappointment and dejection. Attempts to make this human interaction free of any risk would almost certainly render human interaction meaningless. But when there is no common understanding of what role sex has in our lives, then people are much more likely to get hurt much more often, not just psychologically but physically. And in patriarchy, those injuries will be endured mostly by women and children.

An example: Perhaps one person believes sex can be about physical pleasure, after which two people can part without sustained emotional connection. Another person sees sex as a more emotional experience that creates a bond between two people. If they meet, are attracted to each other, and engage in sexual activity, their conflicting notions of what sex is for will create emotional stress. We can brush that off as "that's the way it goes," but why ignore such a common problem? Why not seek greater understanding that can lessen the degree and severity of the problem?

Or perhaps the members of one group are socialized to view sex as the acquisition of pleasure by the taking of members of another group. In day-to-day life, the people from the dominant group will act on that understanding of the meaning of sex in ways that routinely will objectify and degrade the members of the subordinate group. No one of the members of the dominant group—okay, let's just call them men—will likely stand up in public and explicitly defend that conception of sex in such direct terms. But so long as the public conversation of the "what is sex for?" question is muted, then those men can act on that conception without having to defend it or be held accountable for it.

So, let's not be so afraid of the conversation. If we start talking more openly and honestly, it's possible we could reduce some of the existing negative aspects of sex and expand a lot of potential positives.

ASKING TOO MUCH OF SEX

I believe that such a conversation about the role of sex, no matter what conclusion any one person reaches, would show us that we are asking too much of sex.

A friend once told me he thought that sex could be many things, including a simple expression of interest in getting to know someone. Sex, he said, "can be like a warm handshake" when two people meet. Sex had been, for him, like that at times. He also said that sex could be something shared exclusively between two people who plan to love each other for a lifetime, and that he had that experience as well. He claimed that the former use of sex had no impact on the latter.

I was skeptical; I think that's a lot to ask of one human practice, to expect it has the ability to carry so much meaning. Can the same set of acts really bear up under that weight? Can we make sense—not in the abstract, but in our everyday lives, where we live—of one practice in so many different ways? If sex can be something as routine as a handshake, engaged in with many people almost without thought, can it also be an expression of our most intense connection to a single person with whom we plan to share our lives? Obviously, people can perform sexually in either mode, as well as many points in between; we see that happening all around us. In a single moment in any one person's life, it may seem to work. But the question is whether such an expansive range of meanings can over time help promote human flourishing in a just and sustainable culture. In other words, if one practice can carry virtually any meaning, can humans engage in that practice with any clarity of connection?

Someone once challenged me on this by pointing out that sex is hardly the only practice about which we could ask these questions and reach such a conclusion, that in fact lots of human activity carries such diversity of meaning without apparent complication. For example, the man said, wine is used both as a recreational drug and a sacrament in Christian communion, and no one suggests that the non-sacred use of it demeans the sacred. It's an apt comparison, but one that reinforces, not undermines, my point.

First, in communion one takes a sip of wine as a symbolic act. When used recreationally, people drink wine by the glass. A sip of wine in communion is symbolic, just as a short kiss between two people can be symbolic. But many in contemporary culture believe that full sexual intercourse can have these multiple meanings, which is analogous to claiming that we could chug a bottle of wine at communion just as one might at a party, and the meaning of the communion wine would be untouched.

But beyond that, we see how the analogy helps us understand the stress we put on sex by expecting it to carry so much meaning. Although people who abstain from alcohol may disagree, wine—and alcohol more generally—has a potentially useful social function in its role as a part of a communal gathering and its ability to put people at ease. Used in moderation, alcohol, some (including me) would argue, can enhance the quality of social gatherings and contribute to human flourishing. We might argue that is what alcohol is for. But in contemporary society, in the real-world way in which people who live with various kinds of stress actually use these beverages, alcohol also easily can be abused in ways that are destructive to both the individual with the drinking problem and the larger society. In part because drinking has come to be used in so many different ways—just as sex is used in so many different ways—people have difficulty making sense of how to negotiate this range of uses and meanings. In the same sense, we are asking the practice of consuming alcohol to carry too much meaning, and the result is that an act that can be positive routinely produces extremely negative consequences.

Different people will have different abilities to negotiate the expanded range of meaning, but still patterns will emerge. For example, ask any group of heterosexual women, and I am confident that the majority will be able to describe some damaging experience that resulted from differences between their answer to the question "what is sex for?" and men's answers. That doesn't mean every heterosexual man has spent his life locked into a particular conception of sex that is always in opposition to every heterosexual woman's conception. I simply am observing patterns, which is the basis for making choices about the complexity of social interaction.

My point here can be summarized in something a male friend once told me. "My sex life is great, but my love life stinks," he said, somewhat forlornly. In his life, he had no shortage of sexual partners who could satisfy a certain kind of need for physical pleasure. But that activity was not fulfilling another equally powerful need, for intimacy that could be expressed sexually but also went beyond sex. Here, the consequences of asking sex to carry so much meaning were clear not in tension between people, but inside a single human being. While he hoped sex could be a point of connection with someone he loved, he continued to have sex in ways that sometimes included no connection to the other person.

SOME THOUGHTS ON WHAT SEX IS NOT FOR

Any attempt to start a conversation about the meaning of sex often prompts a reflexive rejection of the possibility of such a conversation, as if it can only result in the arbitrary imposition of sexual rules. As one prominent pro-pornography feminist scholar put it in an interview, "Really, who are [anti-pornography activists] to tell us where our sexual imaginations should go?"[1]

I agree. No one can really tell anyone else where their sexual imaginations should go. Imaginations are unruly and notoriously resistant to attempts at control. But our imaginations come from somewhere. Our imaginations may be internal in some ways, but they are influenced by external forces. Can we not have a conversation about those influences? Are we so fragile that our sexual imaginations can't stand up to honest human conversation?

I have no interest in telling people where their sexual imaginations must end up. But I would like to be part of a conversation about the direction in which we think our sexual imaginations can move. My interest isn't motivated by a desire to impose on others but to learn from others. Rather than wall myself off from such a conversation, I wish it were more common. I think that conversation has to start with the sexual troubles we find ourselves in, which for me means starting with men and their desires.

One of the common discussions men have—and one that perplexed me even before I had any critical consciousness around these issues—is about what kind of bodies and body parts they like and what specific sex acts they enjoy. Men frequently say things such as "I like women with big breasts." Others will say they like small breasts. The point is not the particular size preferred, but the fact that men will state a preference independent of any particular woman. They are not talking about the experience of meeting a specific woman and finding some aspect of her appearance attractive, but instead about a generic preference. The physical feature can be hair color or length, height, weight, size of a butt, shape of the calf—virtually anything, sometimes down to rather minute details. This is not, in my experience, unique to heterosexual men; I've heard gay men talk in similar fashion.

But how can I know what I will find attractive in the abstract? To talk about what I like sexually, detached from a real person, is to admit that sexual acts can be detached from a real person. It's a way men acknowledge that they can function sexually outside of a relationship, isolated, alone in their fantasies. Again, there's nothing wrong with acknowledging that we are complex animals, that we fantasize, that our sexuality is mysterious in ways we can't fully understand. But that's not the same as collapsing into an isolated world in which we begin the process of engaging sexually by reducing a potential partner to body parts. This goes beyond objectifying a person; it's the process by which men turn women into their body parts.

I know there are psychoanalytic theories about fetishes that will explain objectification, if only I would take more time to understand them, or perhaps if only I were sophisticated enough to understand them. I've tried, but in the end I still come back to a sense that there is something dangerous about the process. As a person, I find something sad about it. Whatever the complicated psychological explanations various people and schools of thought may have to offer us, we can't avoid what these things say about us as a people.

Again, to be clear: Certainly different people will find different things attractive; we are not robots, after all. There do emerge in cultures some standards of beauty that are common, but there also is considerable individual variation. My interest is not in imposing a conception of what is beautiful or sexually alluring on anyone. My point is that men (and women, too, but my experience is that this is much more common among men in contemporary society) will make such declarations in the abstract, about women's bodies in general.

I think this point also can be summarized in one comment I once heard a man make. During a discussion of sexual experiences that included reflections on negative experiences people had had, he said, "There's no such thing as a bad orgasm." I assume that he meant getting off was getting off—no matter what the circumstances or methods, it was always good. But there are, of course, bad orgasms. There are orgasms that hurt people, mostly women and children. There are orgasms that keep men cut off from themselves.

The man's comment, while hyperbolic, reflected a common view of sexuality in men I have known: That while sex has an emotional component, in the end getting off is always a good thing. The assumption behind such a view is that whatever else we may layer on top of sex, the core reality of sex—what really matters—is that it's about physical pleasure. For those with such a view of sex, it's not surprising that pornography is popular. It works. It delivers that orgasm. Once one has accepted that understanding of sex, the quest for the best pornography to deliver that orgasm with the most intensity takes precedence, and other considerations—about the costs to the people who make pornography, the politics of the images, or the harms that may result from the industry—drop out of sight.[2]

SOME THOUGHTS ON WHAT SEX MIGHT BE FOR

In the debate over sexually explicit images, many people have distinguished between patriarchal pornography and erotica that is rooted in egalitarian and/or feminist values. Erotica is taken to be that which can spark an erotic sensibility or power within us that is deeper than pornographic pleasure. While much of what is labeled erotica seems to me to be pornography with slightly higher production values, the concept of the erotic is useful in thinking about the role of sex in human life.

But "erotic" should not be seen as merely a synonym for "sexual activity." An influential essay by the late poet Audre

Lorde reminds us that we should not fall into the trap of falsely cordoning off women's erotic power in the bedroom, where it is so often made into "plasticized sensation," and easily confused with the pornographic. For Lorde, the erotic is a life force, a creative energy: "Those physical, emotional, and psychic expressions of what is deepest and strongest and richest within each of us, being shared: the passions of love, in its deepest meanings."[3]

Lorde writes about expressing her erotic power in some ways that the culture does not define as sexual and others that the culture might call sexual; she writes of the erotic power flowing both in the act of writing a good poem and in "moving into sunlight against the body of a woman I love." Whatever the expression of that erotic power, what matters is that "recognizing the power of the erotic within our lives can give us the energy to pursue genuine change within our world, rather than merely settling for a shift of characters in the same weary drama."[4]

When I have talked about the quest to transcend that weary drama, people have often asked me what kind of sex acts I imagine will connect us to our erotic power. I always hesitate to respond, not simply because I'm unqualified to offer a sexual recipe book to people, but because I think it is the wrong question. It's not a question of specific acts as much as it is a question of how we relate to each other. Toward the deepening of our understanding of self, other, and sex, I have found two other distinctions helpful: magic vs. mystery, and heat vs. light.

People often talk about sex as being magical, imbued with a capacity to take partners to some higher state of consciousness. A more formal sense of "sex magic" in various traditions attempts to turn sex into a spiritual ritual of sorts, though most people use the term "magic" or "magical" to describe something short of a sacred rite. I find "magic" to be an unfortunate term to use in connection with sex, because it implies the act can be understood.[5] Though "magic" is used to describe things that most people don't understand, magic is a process that can at least potentially be understood. When magicians perform magic tricks, we may not at first understand how they were done, but we know that the magicians understand and that we could, with enough study, figure it out for ourselves. Magic depends on misdirection, on the performer training our attention away from the secret of the trick.

I don't think of sex as magic, as something one can ever really learn. Rather than conceptualizing sex as tricks that can be analyzed, sex is more mystery, something beyond our capacity to understand. When we feel truly connected to another person and express that sexually—when we truly touch another person—it isn't really magic; it's not something we can fully grasp. It is mystery, and it is that mystery—or the hope we can connect to that mystery—that keeps us alive sexually. Without it, our sexual lives tend to fall into routine. Though magic can be entertaining, even it can become routine.

Another common way people talk about sex, especially in the past decade, is in terms of heat: She's hot; he's a hottie; we had hot sex. In the world of hot, it's natural to focus on friction, which is what produces heat. Sex becomes bump-and-grind; the friction produces the heat, and the heat makes the sex good. There are plenty of books on the subject, including a series by Tracey Cox, who describes herself as "an international sex, body language and relationships expert."[6] She began in 1998 with *Hot Sex: How to Do It* and continued with *Hot Relationships: How to Know What You Want, Get What You Want, and Keep It Red Hot!*; *Hot Love: How to Get It*; and *The Hot Sex Handbook*. In 2006, she increased the temperature with *Superhotsex*. Welcome to a world in which everyone is hot and happy.

But we should take note of a phrase commonly used to describe an argument that is intense but which doesn't really advance our understanding; we say that such an engagement "produced more heat than light." As someone who grew up on the frozen prairie of the upper Midwest, I'm aware of the need for heat to survive, but in terms of expanding our understanding of self and other, it seems that light is more helpful than heat.

So, what if our sexual activity—our embodied connections—could be less about heat and more about light? What if instead of desperately seeking hot sex, we searched for a way to produce light when we touch? What if such touch were about finding a way to create light between people so that we could see ourselves and each other better? If the goal is knowing ourselves and each other like that, then what we need is not really heat but light to illuminate the path. How do we touch and talk to each other to shine that light? There can be no recipe book for that, no list of sexual positions to work through so that we may reach sexual bliss. There is only the ongoing quest to touch and be touched, to be truly alive. James Baldwin, as he so often did, got to the heart of this in a comment that is often quoted: "I think the inability to love is the central problem, because the inability masks a certain terror, and that terror is the terror of being touched. And, if you can't be touched, you can't be changed. And, if you can't be changed, you can't be alive."[7]

But what about when touching becomes, well, boring? A friend raised this question. This talk about mystery and light is all well and good, she said, but in the real world it's not so easy to keep sex in such a lofty position. People in long-term relationships may have kids, jobs, and other stress in their lives that may lead their sex lives to become routine and unsatisfying for one or both partners. In such a situation, why not use an outside stimulus such as pornography to jump-start the sexual aspect of the relationship?

The question is important, in part because so many people face exactly that situation, but also because it reinforces my point. When sex becomes, in this formulation, boring, when a couple even stops having sex, why must we assume that the goal is to immediately resume sexual activity? If the goal is intimacy, sex is not the only route to that. If for some reason the sexual path to that connection is no longer open in the way a couple has known it in the past, would not a period of trying to understand that change be appropriate? Before prescribing a treatment, such as sexually explicit media, would it not be better to spend some time on the diagnosis? In a culture that is compulsively sexual in public, it's not surprising that people feel the need to be constantly sexual in private. We can understand sex as a natural and healthy part of human existence and also understand that it also can be healthy for people to go for periods of time without being sexual.

When one doesn't rush to reestablish sexual activity, other ways of knowing another person and oneself have time to emerge. For example, couples whose frequency of intercourse or genital sex drops often find that a sense of intimacy can come from other ways of touching that typically aren't thought of as sexual but can take on an erotic and sexual quality. Couples may also find out that not immediately rushing to re-create an established pattern of sexual behavior can create new space for talking, which can lead to a new sense of connection.

Whatever one's personal preferences for various kinds of talking and touching, it's clear that our decisions around sex and intimacy are based on some decision we have made—whether conscious or not—about the role sex plays in human life. So, we're back to the question: What is sex for?

BEYOND PLEASURE

Obviously, there can be no one answer to such a complex question. But what would it mean in a culture obsessed with sexual heat to suggest that we think a bit about what it might mean to truly touch, to touch lightly, to touch with light? What would it mean to accept that there is inevitably a mystery to sex that we should acknowledge and honor? If we were to do that, what might we feel? What might we see? Where might it lead us?

I think that path leads to a place beyond pleasure and toward joy.

That requires some definitions. By suggesting that we need to go beyond pleasure, I am not suggesting that feeling good is a bad thing, that the pleasures of our physical bodies are suspect. Indeed, feeling alive in one's body requires the ability to feel those pleasures—of exercise and play, the taste of good food, the sound of music, and touch. But "pleasure," in the sense of purely physical sensations, does not meet our needs in the same sense as does the experience of "joy," in the sense of a deeper experience of the mystery of sex.

When I hear men say "there's no such thing as a bad orgasm," I understand how that physical experience always has a pleasurable aspect to it, no matter what the circumstances. But are all orgasms joyful? If forced to choose between a known pleasure and the more complex, shifting, uncertain terrain on which we might find joy, where will we land?

I have experienced pleasure in my life. For me, pleasure has been a mixed bag. It feels good, but it often doesn't feel like enough. I have experienced joy in my life. For me, joy is pretty much always a good thing.

The pornographic culture is obsessed with pleasure, which is seductive. But it misses the essence of Baldwin's warning about the inability to love. In that same interview, he prefaced his remarks about the fear of being touched with this comment:

"The great difficulty is to say YES to life. The difficult quest is to be oneself, to be true, to say YES with courage—to accept one's sexuality, one's race, one's bittersweet contradictions."[8]

Life is, indeed, bittersweet contradictions. It is suffering and joy. We struggle to build the strength to come to terms with the inescapable fragility of life.

Maybe, just maybe, sex is a part of that struggle. Maybe that is what sex is for.

masculinity

[WHAT CAN MEN DO?]

This final chapter, asking what we should and can do about issues raised by the feminist critique of pornography, is directed specifically at heterosexual men. Many of the facts and arguments throughout this book are no doubt relevant to women, but I see my task as a man to be primarily to speak to other men. And while much of what I say may be of value to gay men in thinking through their relationships, the discussion will be focused on heterosexual men.

I take a roundabout way to discussing appropriate actions because, when presented with a cogent critique of pornography, many people rush to ask, "What can we do?" If pornography were a simple problem that could be isolated from a larger set of issues about contemporary culture, perhaps there might be an easy answer to that question. But that's not the case, which is why this book sets the question of pornography within the larger question of masculinity. In my experience, when men are confronted with these issues, it's tempting to want to identify actions immediately, in part to avoid coming to terms with the depth of the critique. I know, because I did that for years.

So, before we move to act, let's stop to take time to make sure we understand. The desire to act, to make the world a better place, is a healthy instinct; such action is obviously necessary if we are to imagine a decent future—or any future—for human beings on this planet. But it's also crucial to act with a full analysis, with a deep understanding of the nature of the problems we face. So, before talking about action, let's make sure we have truly faced the question and faced ourselves.

Our conception of justice includes a conception of gender justice, of overcoming the deeply rooted sexism of contemporary society. The intensity and form of that sexism varies from place to place, but there is virtually no space on the planet free from it. In this book, I have tried to articulate why the support and use of pornography is inconsistent with general principles of justice and how pornography is a misogynistic and racist enterprise that supports instead of challenges patriarchy.

If a man accepts that conclusion, and if he actually believes in the principles that he claims to hold, the most obvious action is that he should stop using women through the sexual-exploitation industries—prostitution, pornography, strip bars, phone sex, massage parlors. Men should do that because there is a compelling argument from justice, because it's the right thing to do.

But we can observe that people in positions of power and privilege do not always act in ways consistent with principles of justice. Arguments about what is right do not always carry the day with people who, if they were to do the right thing, might lose something they value for themselves. This is certainly the case with pornography and sex. For many men, the sexual-exploitation industries deliver to them something of value (an orgasm). Beyond those specific kinds of commercial sex transactions, many men believe that retaining a position of dominance and control in relationship to women in other relationships, whether intimate or not, has value for them.

So, if we are to fashion not only an argument rooted in justice but also an argument rooted in self-interest, the task is to explain to men why giving up those commercial sexual transactions and striving to achieve greater equality and power sharing in our lives is a good thing—for men. Much of this book has laid out the argument that whatever benefits men derive from the dominant conception of masculinity, they come at a huge cost; we never feel man enough, and hence remain in an uneasy state in relation to ourselves, other men, and women. I have argued that when we objectify women and use sex as a way to feel power over women, we reduce the richness of intimacy and experience sex primarily as a quest for an ultimately unfulfilling, narrowed sense of physical pleasure.

From that somewhat abstract level, I want to talk in more specific detail about the emotional realities of using pornography, in an attempt to go deeper into men's struggles. And then I want to put those emotional questions back into political context, to make sure we stay focused on the question of justice, for all.

SHAME AND GUILT

One of the most noticeable changes over the past three decades in the way men use pornography is the level of openness with which they discuss it. When I was a young man, the ways we acknowledged pornography use to other men was complex. As children, a lot of pornography viewing was in groups, in part because the magazines were available but still a rather precious commodity, and hence shared. As we grew older, there were some collective outings to see pornographic movies and some group viewing of magazines, but by that time much of our pornography use was solitary, and primarily to facilitate masturbation.

As teenagers and young adults, we all knew we were all doing it, but we didn't talk much about it. That was in part because pornography use was always double-edged. On the one hand, it was a guy thing that we all did; to use pornography was to be one of the boys. Yet open acknowledgment of the use of pornography as a masturbation aid left one open to possible ridicule, especially once boys reached the age when sex with girls was plausible (sex with other boys was equally plausible, of course, but unacceptable to acknowledge). We had to be careful about how openly we talked about pornography use, lest another boy use our admission against us by suggesting that we masturbated to pornography because we "couldn't get any," meaning sex from a woman. At the same time pornography use helped define you as a man, it also could be turned against you as proof you weren't man enough.

On this front, things have changed. For many men today, open and explicit talk about pornography is common. Howard Stern—the radio/television host whose talk show regularly features pornography performers—and his imitators have made it common fare in mainstream media. No doubt many men still feel conflicted and hide their use of pornography, especially from female friends and partners who may disapprove, but for men to acknowledge that they regularly use pornography is no longer so fraught with the same danger. In short, for many men, it has become the norm.

Although its use is more out in the open, I'm not sure men using pornography today totally escape the struggle with shame that many of my generation remember, or still experience. In an earlier chapter I talked about the cycle of men being attracted to pornography because of the intensity of the sexual experience it provided, in a context that doesn't require us to be open, and hence vulnerable, to a sex partner. After orgasm, many men feel that shame. That shame can lead to a declaration to oneself not to use pornography again, which typically is abandoned the next time the desire for a sexual feeling without the complications of another person arises. That cycle can go on indefinitely. To paraphrase Mark Twain on smoking, many men might say, "Quitting pornography is easy—I've done it hundreds of times."

I'm not suggesting that is how all men experience pornography, but that basic pattern was very much my experience, and I have heard it from many other men over the years. Pornography use produces in men a very conflicted sense of self and sex, as seen in a comment from one of the self-identified pornography users I interviewed in a study in the early 1990s. At the time of the interview, the man was a 34-year-old heating-and-refrigeration repairman, who spent much of his work day driving from one job site to the next, which presented him with the opportunity to drive past pornographic shops. Even when he had no conscious plans to visit one, he said:

> It's like a fucking bee line to the [adult book-store]. I'll be thinking about something else and driving along, and all of a sudden there the fuck I am, sitting in front of the place. I've felt like, you know, why control it. Just fucking do what you want to do, and whatever. Pretty much constant my whole life. I think sex is fun and sex is good, stuff like that. I don't see anything wrong with that at all.

That comment captures much of the internal turmoil that many men experience. Pornography use can have addictive-like qualities,[1] and the desire for that rush of intensity that pornography provides can seem to overwhelm one's ability to make conscious decisions. In the face of the power of those images, it's tempting to resolve the tension by suppressing it, by adopting the attitude that "porn is harmless fun," not only with others but with oneself.

The problem, of course, is that the internal tension is not so easily erased. Pornography's defenders often argue that this tension is simply a by-product of a sexually repressive culture, and no doubt for some men a history of sexual repression, often rooted in religious ideology, can play a role in their feelings of shame. But from my experience—and, again, from similar experiences reported by other men—I see another process at work: the recognition that turning women into objects on a page or a screen in order to feel sexual pleasure is unhealthy for everyone, that it demeans everyone. After two decades of listening to men speak about this, I believe that many of us—no matter what we say in public or to ourselves—at some level understand that such a sexuality and such a use of women is inconsistent with building a decent world based on our common principles of justice. We know it, as much through our emotional experiences as through rational thought, and that knowledge bedevils us, leading to shame.

That knowledge is important, but the shame is counterproductive and undermines our ability to find our way clear. To help in that process, I want to suggest that men work to replace that sense of shame with a sense of guilt.

At first glance, that may seem like a nonsensical statement, given that the terms "shame" and "guilt" are often used interchangeably. I won't attempt a full philosophical or psychological analysis, but instead point to a common distinction made between the two—"shame" names the feeling that one *is bad*, while "guilt" describes the recognition that one *has done a bad thing*. In this sense, shame is destructive because it can so easily lead to a self-loathing that hinders a person's emotional development. If one believes oneself to *be bad* in some intrinsic sense—as if it is a part of one's self—then it becomes difficult to imagine modifying the bad behavior, since it arises from an intrinsic failing. Shame, in this sense, is always a negative.

But guilt is more complex. It's a positive aspect of human psychology to be able to recognize when one has engaged in an act that is contrary to one's own moral and/or political principles, especially when that act injures another. Without the capacity to recognize that gap between who we say we are and how we behave, it's difficult to imagine individuals or societies making moral and political progress, toward a more just world. In that sense, guilt is a necessary part of the process of acknowledging our mistakes, being accountable for them, and moving forward. Yet it's also possible to feel excessively guilty, to focus on one's mistakes in an unbalanced fashion that leads not to action but to a kind of emotional or moral paralysis.

So, shame tends to keep us locked in dysfunctional behavior, while guilt can be a step toward accountability for past actions and change in the future. If we reject shaming men about their use, misuse, or abuse of women, we need not reject the positive role of guilt, which can be a productive part of a process by which one comes to see that an action was morally unacceptable and by which one can rectify, to the degree possible, injuries done to others and begin the process of ensuring the bad action is not repeated.

MEN DON'T ALWAYS FEEL POWERFUL, BUT MEN ARE NOT OPPRESSED

This distinction between shame and guilt can help us negotiate another important emotional reality for men that feeds into pornography use—a sense of powerlessness. Just as we have to distinguish between shame and guilt, it's important here to distinguish between an individual man's experience of powerlessness and the claim that men are oppressed. Men often feel powerless, sometimes for reasons that are justified and other times for reasons that are self-indulgent, but it's important to be clear that men are not oppressed as men. Here again I want to work from my own experience and the pattern that I have observed after nearly two decades of listening to men.

We need to start with an understanding of oppression, a concept that focuses not on any individual's feelings but on the nature of a system. Marilyn Frye defines oppression as "a system of interrelated barriers and forces which reduce, immobilize and mold people who belong to a certain group, and effect their subordination to another group (individually to individuals of the other group, and as a group, to that group)."[2] Oppression, then, is not about any one experience of an individual but a pattern of experiences that affect people because of their identity as part of a group. From there, we can start to understand the nature of men's struggles as members of a group that oppresses women, even though we don't always experience ourselves as powerful.

Because no man ever meets all the criteria of being a real man, it's inevitable that men will often feel powerless. When I was a small, skinny kid being taunted by stronger boys, I felt powerless, and indeed I was. In that setting, I lacked the ability to control a situation and was, by virtue of my size, at the mercy of bigger boys who used that greater strength to gain sadistic pleasure at my expense. As I grew up, I found myself in many situations in which I didn't have much power, typically because of my age or class status. Other men who had even fewer privileges than I do, especially as a result of their class and race, no doubt feel powerless in situations in which those aspects of their identity or status put them in a vulnerable position. Such experiences are real and are often tied to other systems of oppression, most notably white supremacy, class dominance, and heterosexism.

But men also describe feeling powerless when they feel that their inherent "right" to control others is undermined. For example, I have heard men complain that their kids don't listen to them or their wives will no longer have sex with them, and that they feel powerless to deal with the situation. The first question for these men should be, of course, why? Why don't your kids respect you and why does your wife avoid sex? Perhaps it has something to do with the presumption of a right to rule and dictate?

So, men's feelings of powerlessness may be the result of a system of oppression such as racism, when men of color are treated as less than fully human in a white-supremacist system. When a black man is stopped by police for no reason other than being in a white neighborhood—for "driving while black"—that man is experiencing racial oppression. He is facing that system of interrelated barriers and forces as a person of color. But when a man feels powerless because his presumed right to status as a man is not respected in some way he feels it should be, that's not oppression. That's simply a reminder that when people have unearned privilege and power, they are more prone to being self-indulgent and whiney.

But men also suffer real injuries when they are targeted by other men in that King of the Hill game. These experiences are not trivial. But it's misguided to call it oppression. When we speak of oppression, we speak of a class of people who impose a system on others. In gender terms, men oppress women. What does it mean to suggest that men are oppressed in patriarchy? Are we suggesting that men oppress men? Or that men oppress themselves? Within patriarchy, men reap material and psychological benefits in various ways, depending on their social location. Not all live on top of the hill, literally or metaphorically. But, as Marilyn Frye puts it:

> When the stresses and frustrations of being a man are cited as evidence that oppressors are oppressed by their oppressing, the word "oppression" is being stretched to meaninglessness; it is treated as though its scope includes any and all human experience of limitation or suffering no matter the cause, degree or consequence.[3]

The concept of oppression is important because it helps us understand the systematic nature of discrimination and violence. Within any oppressive system, the class of people on top (men, in this case) won't all have the exact same experience of being on top. In the case of gender, some men will have only very limited access to patriarchal power by virtue of being in another class of people who are the victims of an oppressive system, including race and economic status. And those men who don't fit the dominant conception of masculinity will at times struggle in a position of relative powerlessness compared with other men. We live in a system that advantages men, but that does not mean that men's lives are always so great. But that doesn't change the basic nature of the patriarchy.

These distinctions are important if we are to understand how to fight oppressive systems and create a more just world. Consider this example: A woman with a college degree is a manager of an office in a corporate enterprise in which men and women work at basic clerical and warehouse tasks. The manager can be harsh and unpleasant, sometimes threatening or denigrating employees to get more work out of them. In such situations, men often report feelings of powerlessness, resentment, and anger. The powerlessness is easy to understand; in corporate capitalism, employees have no power and are often treated as mere cogs in a machine designed to maximize the output. It is a system that creates a hierarchy and legitimates the illegitimate power one class has over another. Traditionally the positions of power within that economic system have been held by men, but simply putting a woman in the same job in the same system doesn't change the nature of the system—it remains hierarchical and abusive. The powerlessness is real, because there is an oppressive system in place that creates and maintains the unjust distribution of power.

So, the question is what to do with the legitimate resentment and anger men might feel in that situation. Certainly it's appropriate to hold managers, whether men or women, accountable for any abusive behavior, no matter what the system in which they are working. Perhaps directing some of that anger and resentment at those people—the immediate, front-line face of the oppressive system—is unavoidable, though we should always be channeling that anger into action to change the system as well. But too often men react to women in positions of power with misogyny, often in sexualized terms. I have heard men in such situations talk about how "I'd like to fuck that bitch and teach her a lesson," for example. That kind of reaction demonstrates that no matter what the class position of a man and woman, men can use the weapon of sexualized violence to attempt to assert their dominance.

Not only is such a response ugly and vicious, it's politically reactionary. Instead of focusing attention and energy on the unjust nature of the system, men too often look to use whatever sense of power they do have to lash out at individuals within the system. But the system will change—and the fundamental injustice will be remedied—only when the system is confronted. In that example, we could say that working-class men are oppressed in a system of corporate capitalism. We also could say that those men sometimes try to deal with that by asserting their power as men. No matter how much economic power that female manager has in that setting, in the wider world she is still a woman, subject to discrimination in myriad ways and always facing the threat of sexualized male violence.

These basic concepts are important for us to understand if we are to come to terms with pornography use and move beyond it.

When men are challenged on their participation in the sexual-exploitation industries of prostitution, pornography, and stripping, their common refrain is that it's the women who have the power and the men who are exploited. One male commentator summed up this point of view, which I have repeatedly heard from men for years:

> Women have an opening in their bodies that men need permission to get into and whenever permission is required for something important, the person who gets to give permission has power over the person who has to ask for permission. ... The result of that power imbalance is that women can almost always get some kind of sex when they want it and men cannot do the same thing.[4]

Women might be surprised to learn that they almost always get the sex that they want. But beyond that, let's explore that claim, that somehow men are at the mercy of women, who regulate access to their "openings."

Studies indicate that women prostituted on the street sexually service an average of 1,500 men a year.[5] If we assume these women work six days a week, that would mean they sexually service about five men a day. So, imagine a woman prostituted on the street who is penetrated orally, vaginally, or anally by five different men in a day. Imagine a typical encounter in which a businessman on his lunch hour drives to the "combat zone" in town and negotiates a price with a woman who then performs oral sex on him in his car. He returns to work and she returns to the street. Are we to believe this is a case of women using their power to control men?

Or consider "Dynamite," the woman from the blow-bang video. When that sixth man ejaculates onto her face, is this a situation in which she controls him? When a woman dancing in a strip club bends over to take a dollar bill from a man who proceeds to tell her what kind of sexual acts he would like her to perform on him, is she displaying her power over him?

It is true that in some situations, women who are viewed as sexually desirable can have power over some men, and some women use this power in ways that are manipulative. While men are quick to focus on situations in which they feel relatively powerless, it's important to recognize that women's power in those moments does not automatically extend into power in the wider world of business or politics. And beyond that, let's expand our vision and remember a few unavoidable facts:

> » All women, including those who meet conventional standards of beauty and may have some power to control men through carefully controlling their sexual availability, are at risk of being raped in a culture in which rape is normalized and rarely punished.

> » There are many women who do not meet conventional standards of beauty and never have such power, and who instead must deal with men's rejection of them not only as potential partners but often as human beings.

> » This alleged power is fleeting; as women age in a culture in which men are often obsessed with youth and identify younger women as more attractive, they discover that this power to control men disappears quickly.

So, instead of men focusing on the power they believe women have to control them—using that as a justification for their use of women in prostitution, pornography, and stripping—would it not be more productive to focus on the real power in these sexual-exploitation industries? The men who feel exploited are being exploited in one sense, by other men who profit from the sexual objectification and use of women. There are women in these industries who profit as well, not only through performing but in other roles. But these industries are still dominated by men, and, just as important, all the people in them (male or female) are acting within a hierarchical and patriarchal system in which human needs are subordinated to the desire for material gain and dominance.

Men searching for a sense of sexual fulfillment are being offered a sad substitute for meaningful sexual connection by business owners and managers who are interested primarily in maximizing profit. In this sense, the pornography industry is much like the fast-food industry. McDonald's, Burger King, and the many other restaurant chains that make money by selling mostly high-fat and intensely sweetened food are exploiting people's desire to eat good-tasting food at a reasonable price. These fat-saturated hamburgers and sugary drinks do taste good, if one's tastes have been conditioned to those intense bursts of flavor, and the monetary cost of those flavor bursts is relatively low in the short term. Relentless advertising and sophisticated marketing encourage people to pass by other options for satisfying their hunger (such as learning to cook and eat healthier, tastier foods) and ignore the long-term costs (mostly to their personal health and planetary sustainability). The sexual-exploitation industries are similar. They deliver an intense sexual experience that customers seek at what appears to be a reasonable cost. But by engaging in this method of acquiring sexual pleasure, the male consumers pass by other options for sexual fulfillment (developing deeper connections to a partner or partners) and ignore the long-term costs (to their own emotional well-being, as well as the more dramatic emotional and physical costs to the women).

Wendell Berry, one of the United States' most eloquent advocates for the development of sustainable agriculture outside of predatory capitalism, makes this point when he links food politics with a food aesthetics and ethics. He stresses that one can't be free when one's food sources are controlled by corporations that have interests antithetical to a democratic culture. The result, he argues, is a degradation of all:

> Like industrial sex, industrial eating has become a degraded, poor, and paltry thing. Our kitchens and other eating places more and more resemble filling stations, as our homes more and more resemble motels. "Life is not very interesting," we seem to have decided. "Let its satisfactions be minimal, perfunctory, and fast." We hurry through our meals to go to work and hurry through our work in order to "recreate" ourselves in the evenings and on weekends and vacations. And then we hurry, with the greatest possible speed and noise and violence, through our recreation—for what? To eat the billionth hamburger at some fast-food joint hellbent on increasing the "quality" of our life? And all this is carried out in a remark-

able obliviousness to the causes and effects, the possibilities and the purposes, of the life of the body in this world.[6]

Berry's description of "industrial eating," as he suggests, is also an accurate account of the sexual-exploitation industries, of "industrial sex." In both cases, should we try to deal with the problems of the system by attacking those at the bottom of that system, those with the least power? It may be enticing to think that we can assign responsibility for our own lack of fulfillment to the most vulnerable. But we wouldn't conclude an analysis of the fast-food industry by blaming the teenagers at the restaurant counter for our slavish devotion to foods that are making us unhealthy and obese. So, why should men want to blame the women on the streets, in the films, or dancing in a club for the lack of fulfillment in their sexual lives?

Again, let me stress, the world is complex. To identify sexual-exploitation industries within patriarchy as sexist and counter to basic principles of justice is not to suggest that men are always consciously oppressing women and women are simply victims being oppressed by men without recourse. Despite the caricatures, radical feminists do not make, and never have made, such simplistic claims. Radical feminists focus on a patriarchal system and how various institutions maintain that unjust system of hierarchy.

Before discussing what men can do about patriarchy, there's one more basic point we must stress: There's no escape from responsibility by claiming it is natural.

NATURAL CHOICES

Almost every defense of pornography either implicitly assumes or explicitly asserts that men's desire for sexually explicit material is natural—a result of something specific to men, hardwired, a biological reality, unavoidable and inevitable, no matter how much one might try to change it. It's just the way men are: naturally more visually cued than women, with a natural need for more sex, and a natural capacity for sex without emotion, and so on and so on.

To reiterate points made in earlier chapters: That this kind of male sexual behavior is natural is, at one level, obvious: It happens frequently, and therefore is within men's nature. But is it natural at a deeper level—inevitable in a way that can't be significantly modified and that is somehow essential to the experience of being a man? There's no way to demonstrate that, and plenty of reason to think that if men were socialized differently there would be significantly different patterns of behavior.[7]

In the end, the question of biological determinism is in one sense irrelevant. Even if one could demonstrate that men's aggressive sexual behavior was hardwired and inevitable, so what? If such behavior has consequences that violate our most fundamental sense of justice, would we still not want to do everything we could to prevent it? Would we not in fact work especially hard to overcome that unfortunate reality of our evolutionary history? Would we not look even more skeptically at misogynistic pornography and its potential connection to attitude formation and behavior?

THE PROBLEM OF CHANGING MEN

However we might understand sexual activity, it's clear that it's an important part of being human. Everyone has a sexuality, no matter what they choose to do about it; even celibacy is a sexual choice. So, it's hardly surprising that when people become comfortable with a sexuality that at some level "works" for them, they might be reluctant to give it up. Pornography works for men, in the sense that it produces sexual stimulation that can efficiently lead to orgasm. More generally, male sexuality rooted in a masculinity defined by dominance also works for many men.

Asking men to incorporate a radical feminist critique of masculinity, sexuality, and pornography into their lives is no small request. For most men, taking that critique seriously would mean a major change in how they live. At least, that's what it has meant, and continues to mean, for me. And, as I've emphasized, that change requires introspection that is often painful and can, in the short term, leave one uncertain about the next step. At various times in the past two decades, as my understanding of feminism moves forward, I have felt unsure of how to move forward in my own life. Some of the steps I have taken forward have turned out to be missteps, for which I have had to face the critique of others and cope with my own sense of failure. And taking feminist critique seriously also implies a lifelong commitment to such change, given that there is no easy recipe for how to reinvent oneself as a pro-feminist man and no reason to think one reaches a magical point where one has permanently transcended patriarchal training.

This is the "gift of being made uncomfortable" that feminism offers to men. If one is open to the critique and willing to take it seriously at not only the philosophical and political but also the personal level, then that sense of being uncomfortable with one's own dominant conception of masculinity is inevitable, and struggling with that discomfort will be a lifelong process.

So, if we're honest, the radical feminist critique asks men to begin a process that will (1) hurt, (2) leave you at various points uncertain about how to act, (3) lead to making mistakes for which you will be critiqued, and (4) never end. That's a sales pitch that lacks a certain appeal in a self-indulgent culture of immediate gratification. On top of that, because men are generally in a position of privilege and at this moment there's no strong feminist movement to press these issues, it's extremely easy for men to ignore it all. And that's precisely the response to such a critique the dominant culture supports.

We must continue to present the argument against pornography and patriarchy in terms of justice, but also craft it more clearly in terms of self-interest. Here's the pitch: Letting go of power and privilege—forgoing the material rewards that come with them—offers other rewards. Letting go of the known terrain of pornography and dominance means letting go of the comfort zone within which men can achieve orgasm, but it creates the space in which a new intimacy and sexuality can flourish.

I am against pornography in part because I believe that the rewards of domination, which are seductive, are in the end illusory. I believe that love (based on a commitment to equality articulated in our core philosophies and theologies), compassion (based on our common humanity), and solidarity (based on our need to survive together) can anchor our lives at every level, from the intimate to the global. I believe those things in part because of my necessary faith in "the better angels of our nature," as Abraham Lincoln put it, but also because of my experience. In my life, weighed down as it is sometimes in struggle and failure, I have experienced that intimacy. Once experienced, it's difficult to return to the illusory.

I also believe that to build a world based on love, compassion, and solidarity, we who have privilege and power must be ruthlessly honest with ourselves and each other, in ways that will undoubtedly seem harsh and cause us great pain. We may wish there were another way out, but the lesson of my life is that there is no other path.

The most important choice we have to make is to step onto that path, understandably afraid of where it may lead but safe in the knowledge that along the way we can find our own humanity. It is important to be honest about this: Stepping onto that path has no guarantees. There are too many contingencies in this world to offer glib assurances that these difficult choices lead to the land of milk and honey. We can't know where they lead or what we will encounter along the way. All we can know is where the path of domination leads.

PORNOGRAPHY OFFERS THE PATH TO A DOOR THAT OPENS INTO A PRISON

The pornographers tell us their path leads to an ever-expanding sexuality. One of the central claims of pornography is that it is a gateway to better sex, that it will open up possibilities in our lives. While I can't speak to whether that might be true for some, after 20 years of work on this issue I am confident that pornography's claim is a cruel joke on men.

Pornography claims to take us on a path to a door that will open into more creative erotic space, into imagination, into a garden of sexual delight. Just open this door, pornography tells us, and you will step into a more expansive world. But it turns out that going through the pornographic door typically leads into a prison cell, with four thick walls and no window. It is a dead end. It doesn't give a way to expand our imaginations but a way to constrain them, handing us a sexual script that keeps us locked up and locked down. The pornographers walk away with the money, and we are left with a more limited sense of sex than we started with; we are left with the illusion of pleasure that comes at the expense of joy.

I believe men—even the most boisterous, macho men posturing about sexual conquests—understand that at some level. We understand that the acquisition of pornographic pleasures at the expense of women also comes at the expense of our own humanity. I am not just generalizing from my own experience; this is a consistent theme in my exchanges with men, both in formal research interviews and informal conversation. When most of us strip away our sexual bravado, there is a yearning for something beyond those quick-and-easy pleasures of the pornographic. That is the key to action, to a collective project to change not just ourselves but society.

WHAT MEN CAN DO AND WHAT THE LAW CAN'T DO

I began this chapter promising to discuss action, things that men can do, yet most of the space has been filled with more reflection and analysis. That's appropriate, I think, because we are at an early stage of the movement that will fundamentally change these gender dynamics, and at such an early stage we have to work hard to be clear about what we're up against.

But in the end, we all need to act, both in our own lives and collectively. For men, the first step is realizing that misogyny and the discriminatory practices that flow from it are men's problems. Just as racism and white supremacy are problems of white people, sexism and patriarchy are problems of men, and we have a compelling moral and political obligation to act to eliminate the problem. At the personal level, there are some simple things men can do, starting today:

» Most obviously, we must never use or threaten to use violence against a partner or child. Beyond that, we must examine our behavior for more subtle attempts at controlling the behavior of a partner, such as insulting a partner in a way designed to undermine self-esteem, withholding affection to gain a desired result, or demanding sexual activity in the face of resistance.

» We must stop supporting men who batter, rape, and abuse. Often men talk fairly openly about their abusive behavior. When that happens, we must make it clear that the friendship or work relationship will not be business as usual until the abuse ends and steps are taken to prevent it in the future.

» If we ever have reason to suspect someone is being abused, we must offer support and assistance in whatever way the person can accept.

» We must stop telling or laughing at misogynistic jokes.

» We must stop using pornography, patronizing
strip clubs, or using prostituted women.

» We must remove ourselves from relationships
of domination that institutionalize the subordination of women. When men in our lives
talk of such activity, we must challenge them
to think and act differently.

It's not enough for us to change our personal behavior.
That's a bare minimum. Such change must be followed by participation in movements to change the unjust structures and the
underlying ideology that supports them. The feminist movements in support of this change have lost some of their radical
edge since the 1960s and 70s, but institutions still exist—rape
crisis centers, battered women's shelters, feminist political organizations. All require financial support and volunteer energy,
both of which men can contribute.

All that is fairly obvious. The question most people ask about
the action needed to combat the harms of pornography specifically
concerns the law. Here's a quick primer about the law.

The current law concerning sexually explicit material
comes under the rubric of "obscenity," the category of sexual material that the courts have deemed to be outside full protection
of the First Amendment and subject to regulation by the state
through criminal law. Obscene material is defined as that which
appeals to the prurient interest in sex, depicts sexual conduct in
a patently offensive manner, and lacks serious literary, artistic,
political, or scientific value.[8] The legality of pornography use
depends not only on the nature of the material, but also on the
community and the political climate. Much of what is sold in
pornography shops in the United States fits the definition of
obscenity, but in most jurisdictions prosecutors choose not to
initiate cases, primarily because in many jurisdictions there is
no political support for such prosecutions.

"Indecency" is a term from broadcasting (over-the-air
radio and television) that defines an even broader category that
can be regulated—language or material that, in context, depicts
or describes, in terms patently offensive as measured by contem-

porary community standards for the broadcast medium, sexual or excretory organs or activities.[9]

A separate category is child pornography—material that is either made using children or, in the digital age, made through the use of technology that makes it appear the sexual activity uses children. The former is illegal without question[10]; the status of the second has yet to be completely resolved.[11]

The feminist critique of pornography, growing out of the anti-rape and anti-violence movements, rejected obscenity and criminal law, fashioning instead a harm-based, civil rights legal approach that would have empowered individuals to pursue civil cases for damages when they could prove harm. Rooted in the real-world experiences of women sharing stories through a grassroots movement, that feminist critique highlighted the harms pornography has done to the women and children:

» used in the production of pornography;

» who have pornography forced on them;

» who are sexually assaulted by men who use pornography; and

» living in a culture in which pornography re-inforces and sexualizes women's subordinate status.[12]

This civil rights approach was pursued at the local and state levels with some success and some failure, but ruled unconstitutional in federal court.[13]

There has been extensive debate over the merits and constitutionality of that approach that I won't recount here;[14] I don't want to talk about the law too much because talk about the law tends to derail talk about who we are. Because the pornographers have been so successful at normalizing and mainstreaming their products over the past two decades, we are a long way away from building the understanding that would be required to create appropriate legislative and legal approaches to the harms of pornography and build support for those initiatives. Some day those discussions about law will again be important, but right now too many people want to leapfrog over the difficult work of coming to terms with pornography by instead arguing about the law. I have a suggestion. Let's not talk about the law for a bit. It's not that law is irrelevant; it is and will continue to be an important arena for struggle. But let's talk about the reality of pornography that is ever more cruel and denigrating to women at the same time that it is more widely accepted in our society than ever before. Let's talk about why men can be aroused and achieve orgasm to images of women being treated as less than fully human.

There's an old adage: Allow me to write the stories that people tell, and I will not need to write the laws. The stories that we tell are a powerful force in setting the direction of a society, in shaping our ideas about what it means to be human and a citizen, what it means to be a man and a woman. Pornography is telling us stories about what it means to be a man, to be a woman, to be sexual as men and women. Are these the stories we want told? Is this the world we want to build? If we start seriously asking those questions and struggling to answer them honestly, we may decide that the law is an appropriate tool to build a world rooted in real justice. But first we have to get serious about facing the world that is.

At the moment, it's the pornographers' world. They are the ones telling the most influential stories about gender and power and sex. But that victory is just for the moment, if we can face ourselves and then build a movement that challenges them. We have a lot of work to do.

So, before we debate the meaning of the First Amendment, let's discuss the meaning of a double penetration.

Before we look at the law, let's look in the mirror.

Our Last Glance In The Mirror: The Sad Men

I am at the Adult Entertainment Expo in Las Vegas in January 2006. Once again, at one of the 300 exhibitor booths on the floor of the Sands Expo Center, is Tiffany Holiday, the same pornography performer who had been surrounded by the mob in 2005 in the scene described at the beginning of this book. This time I'm there by myself on a reporting trip, interviewing people for this book. The crowd around Holiday is smaller, only a dozen men or so. She is engaged in the same kind of sexual display as the previous year, simulating masturbation and talking dirty to the guys. But this time there is no critical mass, in numbers or energy. The men carry cameras, camcorders, and cell phones and are even more intent than the previous year on getting the best shot of her exposed body. With no mob to embolden them, the men are reserved, almost polite. They seem no more aware of the humanity of Tiffany Holiday this year than last. But instead of engaging in rowdy, aggressive, hyper-masculinized behavior, they mostly seem timid and nervous.

This is an expression of another side of the dominant masculinity in the United States today. It is the masculinity of a numbed, disconnected, shut-down man, alone, even if there are others around him.

If my options as a man are being part of a mob that is on the edge of violence or being cut off from myself and others, I desperately want to choose something else.

I choose to renounce being a man.

I choose to struggle to be a human being.

endnotes

introduction: masculinity [ANDREA AND JIM]

1   Throughout this book I will use terms such as "normal" and "regular" to describe my experience and the experience of others. I do not mean these terms to indicate "normal" in the normative sense—as a prescription for what should be. Instead, I mean them in the descriptive sense, as experiences that are well within the mainstream of US culture. My goal in this book is, in fact, to challenge the political and moral assumptions behind much of what is taken to be normal in the society.

2   Andrea Dworkin, *Letters From a War Zone: Writings 1976–1987* (London: Secker & Warburg, 1988; Chicago: Lawrence Hill Books, 1993), 170–171.

3   Ibid., 169–170.

4   Ibid., 170.

introduction: pornography [THE PARADOX IN THE MIRROR]

1   Jason Zinomanb, "Debbie's Doing New York Now, but Rate Her PG," *New York Times*, October 27, 2002, Arts and Leisure section, http://www.nytimes.com/2002/10/27/arts/theater/27ZINO.html.

2   Nat Ives, "The 'Playboy' Voter, Comfortably Mainstream," *Advertising Age*, September 6, 2006, http://adage.com/mediaworks/article?article_id=111688.

masculinity: where we are stuck [PLAYING KING OF THE HILL]

1   This is the definition used by the Intersex Society of North America:
    Intersex is a general term used for a variety of conditions in which a person is born with a reproductive or sexual anatomy that doesn't seem to fit the typical definitions of female or male. For example, a person might be born appearing to be female on the outside, but having mostly male-typical anatomy on the inside. Or a person may be born with genitals that seem to be in-between the usual male and female types—for example, a girl may be born with a noticeably large clitoris, or lacking a vaginal opening, or a boy may be born with a notably small penis, or with a scrotum that is divided so that it has formed more like labia. Or a person may be born with mosaic genetics, so that some of her cells have XX chromosomes and some of them have XY.
    Intersex Society of North America, "What is Intersex," http://www.isna.org/faq/what_is_intersex.

2   One prominent researcher reports that the best estimate of the percentage of people born intersexed is 1.7 percent. See Anne Fausto-Sterling, "The Five Sexes, Revisited," *Sciences* 40, no. 3 (2000): 20.

3   *Stanford Encyclopedia of Philosophy*, s.v. "Feminist Epistemology and Philosophy of Science," http://plato.stanford.edu/entries/feminism-epistemology/.

4   Elizabeth Weil, "What If It's (Sort of) a Boy and (Sort of) a Girl?" *New York Times Magazine*, September 24, 2006, http://www.nytimes.com/2006/09/24/magazine/24intersexkids.html.

5   Andrea Dworkin, *Pornography: Men Possessing Women* (New York: Perigee, 1981; New York: Dutton, 1989).

6   Catharine A. MacKinnon, *Feminism Unmodified: Discourses on Life and Law* (Cambridge, MA: Harvard University Press, 1987).

7   Two writers who have been important to the development of my understanding are Marilyn Frye, *The Politics of Reality: Essays in Feminist Theory* (Freedom, CA: Crossing Press, 1983); and Sheila Jeffreys, *Anticlimax: A Feminist Perspective on the Sexual Revolution* (New York: New York University Press, 1990).

pornography: a pornographic world [WHAT IS NORMAL?]

1   Sheila Jeffreys, *The Idea of Prostitution* (North Melbourne, Australia: Spinifex, 1997), 3.

2   See Morality in Media, http://www.moralityinmedia.org/.

3   See National Feminist Antipornography Movement, http://feministantipornographymovement.org/.

4   Marilyn Frye, *Willful Virgin* (Freedom, CA: Crossing Press, 1992), 130.

5   From the Ms. Magazine Project on Campus Sexual Assault, summarized in Mary P. Koss, "Hidden Rape: Sexual Aggression and Victimization in a National Sample of Students in Higher Education," in *Rape and Sexual Assault II*, ed. Ann Wolbert Burgess (New York: Garland, 1988), 3–25.

6   Diana E. H. Russell, *Sexual Exploitation: Rape, Child Sexual Abuse, and Workplace Harassment* (Beverly Hills, CA: Sage, 1984), 285–286.

7   Melanie Randall and Lori Haskell, "Sexual Violence in Women's Lives," *Violence Against Women 1*, no. 1 (1995): 6–31.

8   For an early discussion of this, see Andrea Dworkin, *Woman Hating* (New York: Dutton, 1974).

pornography: pornography as mirror [CONTENT]

1   D. H. Lawrence, *Sex, Literature and Censorship: Essays by D.H. Lawrence* (Melbourne, Australia: William Heinemann, 1955), 195.

2   For the most well-known attempt by feminists to define pornography precisely, see the civil rights ordinance written by Andrea Dworkin and Catharine A. MacKinnon, http://www.nostatusquo.com/ACLU/dworkin/other/ordinance/newday/AppD.htm. The different versions of the ordinance used in various jurisdictions are collected in Catharine A. MacKinnon and Andrea Dworkin, eds., *In Harm's Way: The Pornography Civil Rights Hearings* (Cambridge, MA: Harvard University Press, 1997), 426–461.

3   Andrea Dworkin, *Letters from a War Zone: Writings 1976–1987* (London: Secker & Warburg, 1988; Chicago: Lawrence Hill Books 1993), 264–265.

4   Ibid., 266–267.

5　A snuff film is one in which the murder of a person, almost always a woman, takes place in the context of sex. There are disagreements about whether such films record actual murders or simulated ones. The film called *Snuff* was released in 1976.

6　A short, but necessary, detour on methodology: In the terminology of media research, "qualitative" indicates a close reading, in considerable detail, of a small sample of a media product, in which there are limits to the ways that the results can be generalized to the entire universe of products. "Quantitative" indicates the use of a much larger sample and a coding scheme that, instead of looking at a particular movie in detail and in context, tries to create categories in which attributes of the product can be counted. For example, if one were interested in the nature and amount of violence in a children's cartoon, a quantitative study would define categories of violent acts and count their occurrence in a large number of programs. A qualitative study would focus on a smaller number of shows in order to look more closely.

7　Margaret Baldwin, "The Sexuality of Inequality: The Minneapolis Pornography Ordinance," *Law and Inequality* 2 (1984): 631.

8　Many in the pornography industry would like to change that. Tristan Taormino has written a book and produced two videos under the title *The Ultimate Guide to Anal Sex for Women*, making the argument that women and men can enjoy anal sex if they reject prudish ideas about it and learn to control their muscles. In response to a letter to the "Anal Advisor" on her website, she writes, "When I know that my work has helped someone experience the mind-blowing pleasures of anal sex, I feel that my mission is accomplished" (http://www.puckerup.com/female_pleasure/?&=).

9　Paul Hesky (chief operating officer, Multimedia Pictures), interview with the author at the 2006 AEE.

10　The "Cambria list" advised against the following: shots with the appearance of pain or degradation; blindfolds; wax dripping; bondage or bondage-type toys or gear unless very light; forced sex, rape themes, etc.; degrading dialogue, e.g., "Suck this cock, bitch," while slapping her face with a penis; facials—body shots okay if shot is not nasty; bukkake; spitting or saliva mouth to mouth; girls sharing same dildo in mouth or pussy; peeing unless in a natural setting, e.g., field, roadside; squirting; food used as sex object; coffins; menstruation topics; incest topics; two dicks in/near one mouth; shot of stretching pussy; fisting; hands from two different people fingering same girl; male/male penetration; transsexuals; bi sex; black men with white women themes. Toys are okay if shot is not nasty.

11　This list apparently was intended as a private memo to Paul Cambria's clients that listed types of adult material that had been successfully prosecuted in the past. "The Cambria list eventually became little more than a footnote—or, in some cases, a blueprint for the types of materials upstart studios with in-your-face attitudes should release." Kathee Brewer, "Clean Up Your Act: The Debate Over Self-Regulation," *AVN Online*, July 1, 2006, http://www.avnonline.com/index.php?Primary_Navigation=Editorial&Action=View_Article&Content_ID=270209.

12 Interviewed on *ABC News Primetime Live*, "Young women, porn and profits," January 23, 2003. Although Belladonna was criticized by people in the industry for this interview, she was quickly welcomed back and has become one of the most recognizable performers and directors in gonzo.

13 Tristan Taormino, "Ass to Mouth," *Anal Advisor*, puckerup.com, http://www.puckerup.com/safer_sex/ass_to_mouth/.

14 Ibid.

15 Catharine A. MacKinnon, *Toward a Feminist Theory of the State* (Cambridge, MA: Harvard University Press, 1989), 124.

16 Bobby Manila's Black Attack Gang Bang, http://tour.blackattackgang-bang.com/a/index1.php?np=1&np=1.

17 Gail Dines, "The White Man's Burden: Gonzo Pornography and the Construction of Black Masculinity," *Yale Journal of Law and Feminism* 18 (2006): 296–297.

18 Ibid., 297.

19 JM Productions, *Jerkoffzone.com*, http://jerkoffzone.com/newcatalog/dvdcatalog/americanbukkake3dvd.html.

20 See Linda Williams, *Hard Core: Power, Pleasure and the "Frenzy of the Visible"* (Berkeley: University of California Press, 1989).

21 Bill Margold, quoted in Robert J. Stoller and I. S. Levine, *Coming Attractions: The Making of an X-Rated Video* (New Haven, CT: Yale University Press, 1993), 22.

22 "AVN Directors Roundtable," *Adult Video News*, January 2003, 60.

23 Ibid., 46.

24 "Gape" is the practice of spreading a woman's anus open extremely wide.

25 "Give me gape," *Adult Video News*, September 2004, 158.

26 "Max Hardcore Biography," Max Hardcore official website, http://www.maxhardcore.com/whoismax/index.htm.

27 Home page, Max Hardcore official website, http://maxhardcoreporn.com/front.php.

28 Jeff Steward (owner, JM Productions), interview with the author at the 2005 AEE.

29 Originally posted at GagFactor.com home page, http://www.gagfactor.com/gagfactordotcom.html.

30 "LGI Digital/Sex-Z Pictures: What's in a Name? In This Instance, Everything," *Adult Video News*, August 2006, 97.

pornography: choices, his and hers [PRODUCTION]

1 John Cook, "Venture Capital: Edmond Leaves Online Porn Far Behind," *Seattle Post-Intelligencer*, June 17, 2005, http://seattlepi.nwsource.com/venture/228892_vc17.html.

2 Erik Gruenwedel, "Tricks of the Trade," *Brandweek*, October 30, 2000, 48.

3 Frederick S. Lane, *Obscene Profits: The Entrepreneurs of Pornography in the Cyber Age* (New York: Routledge, 2000), xiv. For a critique of these

estimates, see Dan Akman, "How Big Is Porn?" *Forbes.com*, May 25, 2001, http://www.forbes.com/2001/05/25/0524porn.html.

4   An often-quoted source for this figure is from the website Internet Filter Review. Jerry Ropelato, "Internet Pornography Statistics," *Internet Filter Review*, http://internet-filter-review.toptenreviews.com/internet-pornography-statistics.html.

5   Motion Picture Association of America, "Research and Statistics," http://www.mpaa.org/researchStatistics.asp.

6   Timothy Egan, "Wall Street Meets Pornography," *New York Times*, October 23, 2000, http://www.nytimes.com/2000/10/23/technology/23PORN.html.

7   Jenna Jameson with Neil Strauss, *How to Make Love Like a Porn Star: A Cautionary Tale* (New York: Regan Books, 2004). Regan Books is an imprint of HarperCollins.

8   "State of the US Adult Industry," *Adult Video News*, January 2006.

9   For example, see John Berger, *Ways of Seeing* (New York: Penguin, 1972). Based on a BBC television series, the book demonstrated how European art from the Renaissance forward constructed women as objects to be viewed by men.

10 "Adult Education," *Adult Video News*, August 2006, 58.

11 Jack Morrison, "The Distracted Porn Consumer: You Never Knew Your Online Customers So Well," *AVN Online*, June 1, 2004, http://www.avnonline.com/index.php?Primary_Navigation=Editorial&Action=View_Article&Content_ID=105593.

12 Lucas Mearian, "Porn Industry May Be Decider in Blu-ray, HD-DVD Battle," *PC World*, May 3, 2006, http://www.pcworld.com/article/125618-1/article.html.

13 Randall Crockett, "The Competitive Edge: 1," *Xbiz*, August 16, 2006, http://xbiz.com/article_piece.php?cat=43&id=16550.

14 Club Cytherea, http://www.clubcytherea.com.

15 Margaret Baldwin, "Split at the Root: Prostitution and Feminist Discourses of Law Reform," *Yale Journal of Law and Feminism* 5, no. 1 (1992): 47.

16 Melissa Farley and Howard Barkan, "Prostitution, Violence, and Post-Traumatic Stress Disorder," *Women and Health* 27, no. 3 (1998): 37–49.

17 Melissa Farley et al., "Prostitution and Trafficking in 9 Countries: Update on Violence and Posttraumatic Stress Disorder," *Journal of Trauma Practice* 2, nos. 3/4 (2003): 33–74.

18 For a cogent discussion of this argument in the context of prostitution, see M. Madden Dempsey, "Rethinking Wolfenden: Prostitute-Use, Criminal Law, and Remote Harm," *Criminal Law Review*, 2005: 444–455.

19 John Stagliano, interview, *RogReviews.com*, April 2002, http://www.rogreviews.com/interviews/john_stagliano.asp.

20 Steve C., "A Few Words With Justin Slayer," *foundaymusic.com*, January 23, 2005 http://www.foundrymusic.com/porn/displayinterview.cfm/id/114/div/porn/page/A_FEW_WORDS_WITH_JUSTIN_SLAYER.html.

21 That was a theme in Dworkin's work, and the title of a talk she gave in 1993. Andrea Dworkin, "Pornography Happens to Women," Andrea Dworkin Online Library, http://www.nostatusquo.com/ACLU/dworkin/PornHappens.html.

pornography: we are what we masturbate to [CONSUMPTION]

1 "The Directors," *Adult Video News*, August 2005, 54.

2 Lizzy Borden, who runs Extreme with her husband, Rob Black, described one of their controversial films this way: "A girl being kidnapped, being forced to have sex against her will, being degraded. Being called 'a cunt, a whore, a slut, a piece of shit.' Then being butchered at the end, and spit on. She's being degraded." Borden explained that the woman who performed in the scene was a good friend. "I know she can take it. She's a good actress. And I can abuse somebody that I know, but I can't abuse somebody that I don't know. So it's like, I know that I can hit her harder. ... And at the end I give her a hug, I take her out to dinner, and we go shopping." "American Porn," *Frontline*, February 7, 2002, http://www.pbs.org/wgbh/pages/frontline/shows/porn/interviews/borden.html.

3 Victorio, review of *Buttman's Big Butt Backdoor Babes*, *Adult DVD Talk*, September 14, 2001, http://www.adultdvdtalk.com/reviews/read_review.dlt/sku=1980/buttman%27s-big-butt-backdoor-babes.htm.

4 Johnny Maldoro, "Dirty Pornos: Animal House!" *Village Voice*, November 21, 2002, http://www.villagevoice.com/people/0248,maldoro,40121,24.html.

5 Quoted in Martin Amis, "A Rough Trade," *Guardian*, March 17, 2001, http://www.guardian.co.uk/weekend/story/0,3605,458078,00.html.

6 Berl Kutchinsky, "Pornography and Rape: Theory and practice?" *International Journal of Law and Psychiatry* 14 (1991): 47–64; D. Jaffee and M. A. Strauss, "Sexual Climate and Reported Rape: A State-Level Analysis," *Archives of Sexual Behavior* 16 (1987): 107–123.

7 Neil M. Malamuth, Tamara Addison, and Mary P. Koss, "Pornography and Sexual Aggression: Are There Reliable Effects and Can We Understand Them?" *Annual Review of Sex Research* 11 (2000). 01.

8 Ibid., 79.

9 Michael C. Seto, Alexandra Maric, and Howard E. Barbaree, "The Role Pornography in the Etiology of Sexual Aggression," *Aggression and Violent Behavior* 6 (2001): 35–53.

10 Dolf Zillmann and Jennings Bryant, "Pornography, Sexual Callousness, and the Trivialization of Rape," *Journal of Communication* 32 (1982): 10–21.

11 Diana E. H. Russell, *Dangerous Relationships: Pornography, Misogyny, and Rape* (Thousand Oaks, CA: Sage, 1998), 121.

12 MacKinnon and Dworkin, *In Harm's Way*.

13 Gail Dines and Robert Jensen, "Pornography and Media: Toward a More Critical Analysis," in *Sexualities: Identity, Behavior, and Society*, ed. Michael S. Kimmel and Rebecca F. Plante (New York: Oxford University Press, 2004), 369–380.

14 Mimi H. Silbert and Ayala M. Pines, "Pornography and Sexual Abuse of Women," *Sex Roles* 10 (1984): 864.

15 For an extensive reporting and discussion of these, see Chapter 5, "Using Pornography," in Gail Dines, Robert Jensen, and Ann Russo, *Pornography: The Production and Consumption of Inequality* (New York: Routledge, 1998), 119–134.

16 Ibid., 124.

17 Ibid., 126.

18 Ibid., 128–129.

19 Diana E. H. Russell, "Pornography and Violence: What Does the New Research Say?" in *Take Back the Night: Women on Pornography*, ed. Laura Lederer (New York: William Morrow, 1980), 226.

20 Texas Penal Code, 22.011, http://tlo2.tlc.state.tx.us/statutes/docs/PE/content/pdf/pe.005.00.000022.00.pdf.

21 See A. J. Bridges, R. M. Bergner, and M. Hesson-McInnis, "Romantic Partners' Use of Pornography: Its Significance for Women," *Journal of Sex and Marital Therapy* 29 (2003): 1–14; and R. M. Bergner and A. J. Bridges, "The Significance of Heavy Pornography Involvement for Romantic Partners: Research and Clinical Implications," *Journal of Sex and Marital Therapy* 28 (2000): 193–206.

22 Personal correspondence with author.

23 Susanne Kappeler, *The Pornography of Representation* (Minneapolis: University of Minnesota Press, 1986), 61.

24 Mark, "Why I Am an Anti-Porn Star," One Angry Girl Designs, http://www.oneangrygirl.net/bymark.htm.

25 Bill Margold, quoted in Robert J. Stoller and I. S. Levine, *Coming Attractions: The Making of an X-Rated Video* (New Haven, CT: Yale University Press, 1993), 31.

26 Fertilecelluoid, review of *Fresh Meat*, IMDB, http://www.imdb.com/title/tt0137610/.

27 John Stagliano, interview.

pornography: getting nasty [ARIANA JOLLEE AND LAURA DAVID]

1 Home page of Gag on My Cock website, http://www.gagonmycock.com/home.html.

2 Nina Hartley, "Frustrations of a Feminist Porn Star," http://www.nina.com/vboard/showthread.php?t=656&highlight=Frustrations+Feminist+Porn+Star.

3 Farley and Barkan, "Prostitution, Violence."

4 http://www.ariana-jollee.net/ariana_jollee.htm. Accessed in 2005; site no longer available.

5 Sin City, "Mayhem's Young Bung Debuts with Ariana Jollee at the Helm," February 17, 2005, http://www.sincity.com/news.php?article=02-17-2005.

6 Mike Ramone, "Jollee to Direct for No Boundaries," *AVN Online*, April 28, 2005, http://www.avn.com/index.php?Primary_Navigation=Articles&Action=View_Article&Content_ID=224546.

7 Mike Ramone, "Ariana Jollee: 'The wronger, the better,'" *AVN Insider*, http://www.avninsider.com/stories/lead040804.shtml.

8   "Adult DVD Talker, Skronker Interviews Ariana Jollee," *Adult DVD Talk*, summer 2004, http://www.adultdvdtalk.com/talk/ariana_jollee. asp?.

9   For a description of the filming, see "Ariana Jollee Visits Prague for 50-Guy Creampie," *AVN Insider*, http://www.avninsider.com/stories/ 50guycreampie.shtml.

10   Wikipedia, s.v. "Ariana Jollee," http://en.wikipedia.org/wiki/Ariana_Jollee.

not-masculinity: where we need to go [MORE THAN JUST JOHNS]

1   Bruce David, "Hate Radio," LarryFlynt.com, http://www.larryflynt. com/notebook.php?id=139.

2   Although that is true in my case, given my northern European/ Scandinavian roots and pale skin, it's important to note that some people classified as white have darker skin than people classified as black.

3   This position is explored in depth in John Stoltenberg, *The End of Manhood* (New York: Dutton, 1993).

4   For an example, see "Real Men Don't Rape," the Aurora Center, University of Minnesota, http://www1.umn.edu/aurora/realmendon- trape.pdf.

5   This is the title of a silly book. Bruce Feirstein, *Real Men Don't Eat Quiche* (New York: Pocket Books, 1982).

6   For an example, see http://www.mencanstoprape.org/info-url2698/info- url_show.htm?doc_id=375480.

7   Harvey C. Mansfield, *Manliness* (New Haven, CT: Yale University Press, 2006), 66.

8   For an extended discussion of this, see Andrea Dworkin, *Right-Wing Women* (New York: Perigee Books, 1983).

conclusion: pornography [WHAT IS SEXUALITY FOR?]

1   Linda Williams, quoted in Drake Bennett, "X-ed out: What Happened to the Anti-porn Feminists?" *Boston Globe*, March 6, 2005, http://www. boston.com/news/globe/ideas/articles/2005/03/06/x_ed_out?pg=full.

2   For examples of the way pornography consumers talk about their prefer ences, see http://forum.adultdvdtalk.com/forum/.

3   Audre Lorde, "Uses of the Erotic: The Erotic as Power," in *Sister Outsider* (Freedom, CA: Crossing Press, 1984), 56.

4   Ibid., 59.

5   For example, one can easily find tips on how to make sex magical, es- pecially on the all-important wedding night. Nina Callaway, "10 Sex Tips for a Magical Wedding Night," About.com, http://weddings.about. com/od/bridesandgrooms/a/weddingnighttip.htm.

6   Tracey Cox's official website, "Tracey Cox Profile," http://www.tracey- cox.com/profile.html.

7   James Baldwin, from an interview first published in *The Advocate* and excerpted in the *Utne Reader*, July/August 2002, 100.

8   Ibid.

1   There is an ongoing debate about whether men's habitual and compulsive use of pornography is an addiction in medical/psychological terms, part of a larger controversy over the concept of sex addiction. I proceed on the assumption that research to date does not establish that pornography use should be thought of as addictive in the same sense as drugs such as nicotine, alcohol, or heroin. Hence, my use of the term "addictive-like qualities."

2   Frye, *The Politics of Reality*, 33.

3   Ibid., 1.

4   Peter Cross, "The Truth About Sexual Power," *Buzzle.com*, August 1, 2006, http://www.buzzle.com/editorials/8-1-2006-104125.asp.

5   Cited in Margaret Baldwin, "Pornography and the Traffic in Women," *Yale Journal of Law and Feminism* 1, no. 1 (1989): 123.

6   Wendell Berry, "The Pleasures of Eating," in *What Are People For?* (San Francisco: North Point Press, 1990), 147. This essay can also be found online at http://www.ecoliteracy.org/publications/rsl/wendell-berry.html.

7   See, for example, Peggy Reeves Sanday, "Rape-Prone Versus Rape-Free Campus Cultures," *Violence Against Women* 2, no. 2 (1996): 191–208. She argues convincingly that rape-prone cultures, which force men into proving their manhood through violence, are not inevitable.

8   *Miller v. California*, 413 US 15 (1973).

9   Federal Communications Commission, "FCC consumer facts: Obscene, Profane and Indecent Broadcasts," http://www.fcc.gov/cgb/consumer-facts/obscene.html.

10 *New York v. Ferber*, 458 US 747 (1982).

11 *Ashcroft v. Free Speech Coalition*, 535 US 234 (2002).

12 For a complete account of this approach, see MacKinnon and Dworkin, *In Harm's Way*. For online resources, see their *Pornography and Civil Rights: A New Day for Women's Equality*, http://www.nostatusquo.com/ACLU/dworkin/other/ordinance/newday/TOC.htm.

13 *American Booksellers Assn., Inc. v. Hudnut*, 98 F. Supp. 1316 (S.D. Ind. 1984), aff'd 771 F.2d 323 (7th Cir. 1985), aff'd, 475 US 1001 (1986).

14 For a critique of the ordinance, see Nadine Strossen, *Defending Pornography: Free Speech, Sex, and the Fight for Women's Rights* (New York: Scribner, 1995). For a defense, see MacKinnon, *Toward a Feminist Theory of the State*.

a bibliographic note

Since the publication in 1998 of *Pornography: The Production and Consumption of Inequality*, co-authored with Gail Dines and Ann Russo, I have written for both general and scholarly audiences on this subject. I'm grateful to the editors of those books and publications, including:

» "You Are What You Eat: The Pervasive Porn Industry and What It Says About You and Your Desires," *Clamor*, September/October 2002, 54–59.

» "A Cruel Edge: The Painful Truth About Today's Pornography—And What Men Can Do About It," *MS*, Spring 2004, 54–58. An expanded version of that article appeared as "Cruel to Be Hard: Men and Pornography," *Sexual Assault Report*, January/February 2004, 33–34, 47–48.

» "Pornography and Sexual Violence," VAWnet Applied Research Forum, National Electronic Network on Violence Against Women, July 2004, http://www.vawnet.org/SexualViolence/Research/VAWnetDocuments/AR_PornAndSV.pdf.

» "Empathy and Choices: Rethinking the Debate on Pornography," *American Sexuality*, August 2005.

» "Pornographic Knowledge, the Law, and Social Science," in *Communication and Law: Multidisciplinary Approaches to Research*, ed. Amy Reynolds and Brooke Barnett (Mahwah, NJ: Lawrence Erlbaum, 2006), 87–108.

» "Blow Bangs and Cluster Bombs: The Cruelty of Men and Americans," in *Not for Sale: Feminists Resisting Prostitution and Pornography*, Rebecca Whisnant and Christine Stark (North Melbourne, Australia: Spinifex Press, 2004), 28–37.

» "Pornography and Media: Toward a More Critical Analysis," with Gail Dines, in *Sexualities: Identities, Behaviors, and Society*, ed. Michael S. Kimmel and Rebecca F. Plante (New York: Oxford University Press, 2004), 369–380.

» "Pornography in a Pornographic Culture: Eroticizing Domination and Subordination," with Gail Dines, in *Race/Gender/Media: Considering Diversity Across Audiences, Content, and Producers*, ed. Rebecca Ann Lind (Boston: Allyn and Bacon, 2004), 274–281.

acknowledgments

Perhaps the mark of true collaboration between two people comes when neither can remember where an idea or a phrase originated. On this project, I have two such collaborators, people without whom I could not imagine having written this book. The first is Jim Koplin, whom readers meet in the first chapter of the book. There is no way to describe fully Jim's contribution to my intellectual and political development, starting when I was a clueless bright-eyed graduate student and continuing to my current state as a clueless middle-aged professor. The second is Gail Dines, with whom I have worked on the issue of pornography since we met at an academic conference when we were both junior professors. Since then, I have been happily following Gail's lead, finding it easy to play second fiddle to someone as smart and fierce as Gail.

Dealing with this issue can be emotionally draining at times, but one of the offsetting rewards is the exceptional people one meets in the work. Over the years I have met far too many to list, and at the risk of overlooking anyone, thanks to Dominique Bressi, Ana Bridges, Matt Ezzell, Lierre Keith, Miguel Picker, Chyng Sun, Robert Wosnitzer, Rebecca Whisnant, and the folks at the Illinois Coalition Against Sexual Assault—Carol Corgan, Susan Faupel, Polly Poskin, Denyse Snyder, and Jesse Pierce.

When I first began exploring these issues in Minneapolis in 1988, I was fortunate to meet people who nurtured my emerging interest. Crucial in that period in the community were the women at Organizing against Pornography: Jeanne Barkey, Sally Koplin, and Donna McNamara. At the University of Minnesota, where I was studying, the feminist philosophy reading group was an anchor, particularly Naomi Scheman.

For critical reading and feedback, thanks to Nancy Gilkyson, Jim Rigby, Charles Spencer, Zeynep Toufe, and Pat Youngblood. Finally, special gratitude to Eliza Gilkyson for helping me to live in the world what had previously only been possible in my head.

South End Press is an independent, collectively run book publisher with more than 250 titles in print. Since our founding in 1977, we have met the needs of readers who are exploring, or are already committed to, the politics of radical social change. We publish books that encourage critical thinking and constructive action on the key political, cultural, social, economic, and ecological issues shaping life in the United States and in the world. We provide a forum for a wide variety of democratic social movements and an alternative to the products of corporate publishing.

From its inception, South End has organized itself as an egalitarian collective with decision-making arranged to share as equally as possible the rewards and stresses of running the business. Each collective member is responsible for core editorial and administrative tasks, and all collective members earn the same base salary. South End also has made a practice of inverting the pervasive racial and gender hierarchies in traditional publishing houses; our collective has been majority women since the mid-1980s, and at least 50 percent people of color since the mid-1990s.

Our author list—which includes bell hooks, Andrea Smith, Arundhati Roy, Noam Chomsky, Winona LaDuke, Manning Marable, Ward Churchill, Cherríe Moraga, and Howard Zinn—reflects South End's commitment to publish on myriad issues from diverse perspectives. For more information or to order books, please visit www.southendpress.org.

community supported publishing

Celebrate the bounty of the book harvest! Community Supported Agriculture is helping to make independent, healthy farming sustainable. Now there is CSP! By joining the South End Press CSP, you ensure a steady crop of books guaranteed to change your world. As a member you receive one of the new varieties or a choice heirloom selection free each month and a 10% discount on everything else. Subscriptions start at $20/month. Email southend@southendpress.org for more details.

read. write. revolt.